whither Africa?

whither Africa?

by G. McLeod Bryan

● ● ● ● ● ● ● ● ● ● ●

JOHN KNOX PRESS ● Richmond, Virginia

Library of Congress Catalog Card Number: 61-17110

To
Edna
who gives more to
Africa than I

●　●　●　●　●　●　●　●　●　●

and to
Africa
which has given much
to us both.

Foreword

● ● ● ● ● ● ● ● ● ●

This book is intended to draw the close attention of the Church Universal to what is happening in Africa. Africa is seeking earnestly to redeem her self-respect, having been trodden down over the years by alien nations. She hungers to build democratic governments. She strives legitimately to throw off all trappings, obstacles, discriminations, that bind her to the power of another. In church and state, Africa wants to take its rightful place in the Community of the Nations—to be heard there and accepted as an equal in every way.

Africa calls upon the world to stop all forms of evil discrimination, unjust and inhuman laws, against the indigenes of Africa. The Anglo-Saxon Christian world which encourages these evils must unceasingly be told, without fear or favor, to respect the human dignity of the African, for God who made man made him in his own image and breathed into him the breath of life. The contradictions between what the West professes as its religion— that which it brought to the Africans—and what it practices toward the African must be rectified, and rectified at once. Otherwise the ominous warnings of this writer may become the dire reality of the morrow.

I have known the author as a teacher in my country, as a friend and houseguest. He is an earnest and knowledgeable Christian who has traveled extensively in Africa. His book is the result of careful investigation and is born out of personal experience and sensitivity. The facts have been obtained firsthand. I warmly

7

commend this book to the reading public, particularly to those who would love their fellow human beings whether they be black or white, westerners, Asians, or Africans.

Sir Francis Akanu Ibiam, M.D.
Chairman, All-Africa Church Conference
Governor of East Nigeria

Preface

● ● ● ● ● ● ● ● ● ●

Dr. Aggrey, one of the earliest of the articulate Black Africans, called attention to the fact that the map of Africa forms a question mark. In our day with the storms of ideologies pounding the shores of Africa this symbol is even more pertinent. Which of these ideologies will sweep over these shores, crash the resisting barriers, and finally inundate the land?

In this survey, seven of the ideologies competing for the mind of Black Africa are considered: tribalism, Islam, Christianity, nationalism, racism, communism, and educationalism.

Tribalism is still the innermost psychological spring of action and the major pattern of social organization for the majority of Africans. Its backbone may be broken by the invading forces, but like a snake it lives on and wiggles, thrashing the earth in a fashion even more violent.

Islam is the predominant religion, having had a thousand years' start on any other imported faith and covering the continent from tip to toe. As a political force it has good chances of capturing the bloc-votes in most of the new nation-states where universal franchise is established. Its advantage as a religion is that it provides a socio-political substitute for the culture that it displaces.

Christianity, it may be said, has had its privileged day. For nearly a hundred years, under the aegis of colonial powers, it was the minority religion with the dominant status, almost without competition. Now it faces a pluralistic society, sometimes

9

hostile leaders, and must maintain its foothold as a decidedly minority religion. More and more it will have to depend upon the indigenous witnesses, as white western missionaries may be less welcome in the future.

Nationalism is the new religion of Africa. It is like a rash on the body of Africa. Within this decade more nation-states will have come into existence than at any time in the continent's history, perhaps in the world's history. It is contagious; plague-like it engulfs everyone, everything. Sometimes it is unrestrained and vengeful; occasionally transcendent, universal, and humane. At the moment it is feverish with a realization of its decisive weight in the balance of power in the world.

Racism is like a poisonous plant of Africa which enflames all who come into contact with it. It is not so much a single ideology as a mental disease that shapes the expression of the other ideologies. What is incalculable is the amount and force of resentment which has gradually accumulated against the white westerner and his pretensions.

Communism is naturally interested in perverting nationalism to its own ends. While in the past, communism has been the least appealing and relevant of the alternatives before Africa, perhaps it is the most urgent and plausible in the immediate future. To-day it may seem negligible, tomorrow it may gobble up the continent. What almost happened overnight on the occasion of the Congo independence is a warning.

Africans are frantic to become educated, to use the educational techniques provided by the West. Education has disturbed Africa, and disturbed Africa wants more education. Thus educationalism is part of the new faith of Africans.

In these chapters the concern is not about the material innovations in Africa south of the Sahara, but about the absolute loyalties to which the new African may commit himself. At the moment Africa is like a top wound up by these world tensions, spinning wildly, and nobody knows which way it will fall. Which way, Africa?

Contents

● ● ● ● ● ● ● ● ● ●

Whither bound,
O Africa—
This question mark
Among the nations,
The prize long sought,
Long loved, and never won;
This field
Preserved for God's own
Strange experiments,
This fatherland, this home,
This Africa!
Oh, whither bound?

—DEI ANANG, GHANA

● ● ● ● ● ● ● ● ● ●

You dim-descended, black, divine-soul'd African, large, fine-headed,
    nobly-form'd, superbly destin'd, on equal terms with me! . . .
Health to you! good will to you all, from me and America sent!
Each of us inevitable,
Each of us limitless—each of us with his or her right upon the earth,
Each of us allow'd the eternal purports of the earth.
Each of us here as divinely as any is here.

—WALT WHITMAN

● ● ● ● ● ● ◐ ● ● ●

Here we stand
infants overblown,
poised between two civilizations,
finding the balance irksome,
itching for something to happen,
to tip us one way or the other,
groping in the dark for a helping hand—
and finding none.
I'm tired, O my God, I'm tired,
I'm tired of hanging in the middle way—
But where can I go?

—MABEL IMOUKHUEDE, NIGERIA

13

tribalism

● ● ● ● ● ● ● ● ● ●

While it appears that tribalism has been dealt a death blow by the ideologies invading Africa, this is not to be interpreted as meaning that tribalism will be removed and buried at once. Anthropologists put it this way: "There is no African culture which has not been affected in some way by European contact, and there is none which has entirely given way before it."[1] A man's tribal background usually is still the most important factor in both social and self identity. Also the African's first or basic reaction is most likely to be his tribal tradition, learned in early imitative behavior. The vast proportion of Africans still follow the way of their ancestors with no more than surface modifications. African cultures, contrary to the common notion that they fall like dominoes before the slightest push of westernization, are exhibiting an amazing resiliency and endurance. The new African elite's sudden pride for "the African personality" and his attempt to preserve and cultivate the indigenous values of his culture may further its longevity. The latest anthropological judgment on the persistence of African religion follows: "Despite the intensity of Christian missionary effort and the thousand years of Moslem proselytizing which have marked the history of various parts of Africa, African religions continue to manifest vitality everywhere."[2]

It may be that the hardiness of African tribal culture furnishes a lesson both for Africa and for the world. A big argument over its preservation or deliberate extinction prevails wherever the subject is brought up. Those in favor of its preservation hold that Africa may teach the West something of its own lost glory.

15

Its qualities which make for a solidarity, a loyalty, and a spirit-ual-material wholeness are those which the West has lost to a great extent and which many are struggling to regain. The self-conscious African makes bold to proclaim that his continent could provide an altogether new alternative for human society.

Tribalism as a powerful, enduring, and life-sustaining social system has not been fully appreciated by the outsiders. Africans existed purely to be *detribalized* and then to adopt the ways of *civilized* man. It was a one-way street: all the benefits issued from the white westerner who was bringing the light to the people who sit in darkness. The dark-skinned people of the jungle were depreciated to such an extent that few westerners thought they had anything to add to mankind. The Berlin Conference in 1884 set the mood with its binder that the signatories should "bring home to them the blessings of civilization." A Methodist study book early in this century put it more graphically. On one page was the photograph of an old, bent, and unkempt native, entitled "The Way the African Is," while on the opposite page was a young teacher dressed in white suit and topee, looking for all the world like a black imitation of Teddy Roosevelt, entitled "The Way the African Could Be."

Just as simple as that: clean his body, dress his nakedness in western clothes, teach him diet and health laws, make him liter-ate, and train his hands to clockwork, and presto! the African is better off. But this past attitude toward tribalism is being under-mined. Twentieth-century man is no longer so sure of himself. The awakening African is taking a second measure of "the bless-ings of civilization." Moreover, the newest of the human sciences, anthropology, has taught us to look more carefully at the benefits of other cultures. Finally, Christian thinkers are not quite as dogmatic as David Livingstone who asserted that "neither civili-zation nor Christianity can be promoted alone. In fact, they are inseparable." There is more willingness to grant that Christian-ity may adapt itself to many cultural expressions, including African tribalism. Significant with regard to this was the 1960 contest of the World Dominion organization of British missionaries, offering a prize to the best essay by an African on the subject, "The Africanization of Christianity."

With all this said it still remains that, in the re-evaluation of Africa, the hardest fact for westerners to get into their heads is the lasting value and appeal of tribalism. What does it have to offer, and how can it stand up against the competing ideologies wooing Africans? For a century tribalism has been paraded before the West in terms of witch doctors—eerie moonlit figures dressed in fur capes, antelope horns, and monkey tails . . . savage blacks wildly dancing in their kraals to jungle tom-toms . . . whole villages worked up to the flame-hot pitch of unbelivable sexual orgies . . . all the decencies due to women and children roughly ignored by secret societies of leopard men and blood-thirsty warriors. Tribalism has been depicted as a stagnating, terrorized, disease-ridden society of filthy, illiterate, and scarred-body people. The religion that dominated this backwash of sub-humanity was nothing but superstition, idolatry, and black magic full of witches, ordeals, taboos, charms, divination, and ancestor worship.

Such is the image that flashes before the mind of the average westerner when tribalism is mentioned. If this were the true picture, the hard facts, how then do we account for the longing expressed by many uprooted Africans for a return to the tribal village? A college graduate now occupying the home and position formerly filled by a British District Officer . . . a young lady in the Nigerian Broadcasting Company . . . a Congolese returning from nine years and three degrees in engineering in America —these one and all are able to look the westerner straight in the eye and wish for a return to his tribe. Naturally they are torn between ways of life, and probably possess a romantic, sentimental attachment to the past colored by a brooding nostalgia. But if the description of tribalism given above is accurate, why would they even give it a second look?

Probably no aspect of Africa is more misunderstood than tribalism. (I prefer to speak of tribalism rather than animism, since it seems to me that animism may be a part of tribalism or any other social system, and that tribalism might well continue after animism has been sloughed off. Animism may be transcended in the refined, larger interests of the tribe. While the two most often go together, they need not necessarily.) The early reports of the explorers and of the missionaries exaggerated the ugly side of tribalism. Little good was discovered in it as the cruelty, the superstition, the ill-health, the orgiastic rites, the polygamy, and the labor of women were dwelt upon. It gave rise to the easy formula, "From cannibalism to Christianity." In our day the Mau Mau atrocities in Kenya served to confirm this traditional misconception which was being gradually revised. And it can be added that the current rash of Hollywood movies about Africa is probably doing more to distort our picture of Africa than the self-appointed, swashbuckling explorers and sentimental missionaries ever did.

Our task is to discard the broken-lens spectacles through which we have been looking at tribalism and to try to reach a more seasoned appreciation. We must make a serious effort to secure a more accurate and well-rounded picture of tribalism as a living force organizing the life impulses of a large segment of the world's population. It unquestionably has a survival value equal to if not superior to any other social systems in the world, and it is a powerful alternative at the present moment to competing ways of organizing mankind. That means we must begin by swallowing the pride which is inferred in the oversimplified language of "the savage versus the civilized." We might commence at once by drowning our "civilized" pride in the abandonment of such loose labels as "savage," "heathen," "pagan," and "primitive." (Did not Bishop Sheen recently remind us that we have not *evolved* so far up the scale as to be unkin to the *beast;* rather, the beast resides just within the breast of every person ready to break forth in a growl and to devour.) This does not imply a dumping together of all humans with no meaningful discrimination. It means that we must rid ourselves of the hasty and shallow classifications of human beings which no longer apply. What follows cannot be a tribe-by-tribe account, but gives the more attractive tribal features which generally prevailed. It must not be assumed that tribal life was utopian, but it possessed its own social integrity.

In contrast to the older image of tribalism let us consider a description by an African himself, in this instance a Baganda, writing in 1945 a generalized account of the community he had known:

The idea of community was the chief characteristic in the African society. . . . All distinction was connected with the group in one way or another. The individual had duties to perform for the group, and these had precedence over his private duties. Thus a man might prepare to do some work, but on hearing a particular kind of drumming he would at once leave his work and go and join others to clear the well or the road which led to the chief's house; and on hearing another kind of drumming he would know that there was danger to someone in the neighborhood, and he would go to the rescue. In return the community gave protection to its members. A disabled member was looked after in a most humane way. Co-operation was the rule. . . . Private ownership existed, but just sufficiently to keep the distinction between *meum* and *tuum*—it was not selfish individual ownership, because it might at any time be utilized for the benefit of another. . . . The [extended] family unit was significant not only in economic matters, but also as a real living community. The members by sharing common work, care and experience, grew to know each other so well that there was real affection between the [vast numbers of] individual members. This affection was supplemented by acts of self-sacrifice and natural consideration. If one of their young men wanted to get married, all the other members gave free and enthusiastic support—both financial and moral—in a spirit so generous that there was no room for self-reservation. The more primitive the community, the more abundant were these acts of self-forgetting love. . . . Brotherhood among the Africans was not a limited form. . . . The African society was built on the spirit of helpfulness.[3]

Again, consider the current best-selling autobiography by an African on the far side of the continent from the Uganda society just described, Camara Laye, a French Guinean, first published in 1954 his *L'Enfant Noir* (now in an English paperback entitled *Dark Child*). What was he taught in those hitherto gruesomely depicted tribal initiation rites?

The teaching we received in the bush, far from all prying eyes, had nothing very mysterious about it; nothing, I think, that was not fit for ears other than our own. These lessons, the same as had been taught to all those who had gone before us, confined themselves to outlining the sort of conduct befitting a man: to be absolutely straightforward, to cultivate all the virtues that go to make an honest man, to fulfil our duties towards God, towards our parents, our superiors, and our neighbors.[4]

What about those orgiastic dances of naked savages during full-moon nights? "Most all our dancing was done separately, the men and boys in one place, the women and girls in another." But as he grew up in western schools and towns he wanted to dance with his new-found girl friend, Marie. "Of course we would dance very circumspectly: it is not customary, in our land, to dance in one another's arms: we dance facing each other, but without touching; at the very most we hold hands, but this is not usual. Need I say that, in our shyness, we desired nothing better? But would we have danced together if it had been customary to dance in one another's arms? I hardly know what we would have done. I think we would have abstained, although, like all Africans, we have dancing in our blood."[5]

"Oh, but . . ." the westerner hardened to the old way of thinking of African tribalism will protest. "What do you expect from Africans trying to propagandize for their way of life? They still cannot discount the facts of fifty per cent infant mortality, one hundred per cent illiteracy, cannabalism and internecine wars, periodic starvation, widespread slave trade, polygamy, and the outbreaks of terror. And much of this clothed in religion." Yes, these things must be faced and appraised. As to the fact of these evils being clothed in religion, we have only to look at history throughout the world to realize that some of the worst things ever done on a large scale by otherwise decent people have been done in the name of religion. Primitive religion, like the everyday expressions of so-called higher religions, has both socially cohesive and anti-social practices. No doubt the survival value, the integrity, and the benefits of African tribalism depend greatly upon the importance of religion of the socially cohesive variety. At the same time we must admit the preponderance of anti-social religion: fear of witches, the results of black magic, the loss of life through initiation ceremonies, the use of erratic divination for making social decisions, the dependence upon emotionally unstable persons, etc.

But it is the good in tribalism that we westerners are more in need of seeing. In the present contest for the mind of Africa it is not enough to flippantly dismiss tribalism as "a pagan pastime easily overcome by the intruding forces." Tribalism is still the most solidly entrenched force in Africa, rivaled only by Islam. Living among Africans one can see appealing evidences of it on every hand. For instance, wherever the members of the extended family circle may travel they can always put up on their kinsmen. Hotels and motels have been unnecessary. Yet one can imagine the burden this can put upon a young bourgeois couple having taken up life in a distant city. I cannot forget that during the days I was privileged to reside in the Lagos home of a Nigerian judge, never once did we eat a meal or retire to bed without someone from his tribe back in the bush being present.

Or, again, all the members of the tribe take great pride in the accomplishments of a single member. An African I knew in America met me at an airport in West Africa. Getting my bags to the waiting car, I noticed that it was new. "Felix, how did you come by *this,* when as you just told me you've not secured a job since your return?" He then related to me the incredible account of how his tribal family had met his boat at the docks and had greeted him with the gift of a new car. The car was "his" not in the sense that one belongs to an American suburban family but more like the single automobile owned by one of many fraternity brothers.

On closer observation many commendable features of tribalism emerge. Foremost is the fact of the communal society, where the common life-necessities of all the people are provided for. All share in whatever is available, and while not all share alike there is not much variation. In this relatively classless society *brotherhood* is a reality: all persons who stand in relation to one as an aunt are called "mother," as an uncle is called "father," as a cousin is called "brother" or "sister," as a nephew or niece is called "son" or "daughter." "Home" is always the tribal grounds no matter how far the villager may roam in the world or take up residence somewhere else. The "hearth" concept—often centered around a sacred giant tree in a public clearing—prevails. Sentimental attachment to the home-hearth means that the African, like the patriarchs in the Old Testament, must be carried home for burial. He must dwell in death "in the land of his fathers."

Although there is no absolute ownership and use of land in the individualistic, freehold sense of capitalism, it is wrong to speak of no private property or landholding. A high premium is placed upon the land as belonging to the people, as a gift of God. Theoretically every villager has access to it, to tend his allotted bit. I was informed by uprooted city dwellers living miles from the tribe, that whereas they were not able to secure or to buy land in the city where they resided, they would be *given* land should they desire to build back home.

The solidarity of life is manifest in the daily round of life. Here is a participating society where everybody from the youngest to the oldest shares in the daily routine as well as the gala festivals and ceremonies. Tom-toms soon after four o'clock in the morning awake everybody; all during the day humanity ebbs and flows toward the yam fields, the watering place, the market paths, the hunting territory (depending upon whatever is the activity of the day); on the full moon everybody dances all night. Recreation, like work, is a total affair: there are no spectators, no paid admissions. Art is of the same primary order, where everybody participates, imitates, and creates. Symbols are traditional and are understood as having central meaning. Even the housewife making twenty clay pots in one day will take time to decorate them.

In the ceremonies associated with the life cycle of individuals and with the natural calendar of the work year, the tribe learns the fullness of life. They learn to live with nature, to relax and to conform to her ways, so that the jungle is no enemy. The African tribal life may have endless fears, but there is also an "at peace" with the world of nature which encourages contemplation and quietness. The African lives leisurely. In fact, tribal life knows no mechanical time—which accounts for the hardest adjustment of the African moving into western ways. "Being on time" exposes him to civilized diseases: hypertension, heart attacks, and ulcerated stomach—diseases which heretofore he was virtually without.

In the tribal society the one dream uppermost in the desires of sophisticated western parents is virtually fulfilled: the carefree, uninhibited, idyllic childhood. Swung on the mother's back for two to three years the baby is never allowed to cry, is always breast fed. The traumatic moment comes when it is dropped from the back and allowed to "root hog or die." If it makes that adjustment, it has a blissful span of about ten years with virtually no cares. Initiation rites abruptly bring the puberty-age child into adulthood, with all the burdens of tradition and work thrust upon these new "men" and "women." Needless to say, there is little teen-age problem.

Customary morals are rigidly obeyed. Hence there are no orphans, no unchastity, no prostitution, no divorce, no jails, generally speaking. Social coercion is effective: for instance, old women assigned as "village keepers" expose daring young girls, and if there is a sexual breach the house of the parents may be overturned and burned in certain tribes. Here an elemental justice prevails, rough and crude to western eyes but nonetheless possessing its own jury system, its judges, its witnesses, its precedences, its records (preserved through the profound memories developed by years of reliance upon verbal data), its inviolability, and its swift execution. No jails, but often capital punishment and banishment. Contrary to popular misconception, brute strength alone does not rule, but cunning, shrewdness, and the prowess of weakness is often extolled. A system of law and limited warfare prevails most of the time throughout Africa.

The African's hospitality and personal manners are gracious and sometimes frightfully embarrassing to the cold and casual westerner. Naturally there is ethnocentric narrowness, but I found an openness everywhere—except where the whites had left bad memories of broken relationships. Usually, though, one can count on the most polite and gracious language, and communications and confrontations are gently handled. Nor is a visitor ever left without gifts. He is entertained with the best and is expected to stay as long as he will. Children of the village rarely return without bearing some significant gift to their tribal homefolks. Storytelling is an art, and their proficiency in using the right word and their competence in memory is often amazing. In the open-handed society that prevails in most of the tribes they have learned to cultivate the person-to-person virtues. While there are cases of hosility, intertribal suspicion, and endless warfare on record, Karen Blixen in her tales of Kenya life in the now famous book *Out of Africa* makes the bold claim that African people have more occasion to develop the cosmopolitan point of view than almost anybody in the whole world. This is mainly because they daily encounter so many representatives of different cultures.

In the light of the foregoing assets, it is no wonder that the Baganda tribesman earlier quoted should conclude:

"Such was the community upon which the modern influences of civilization and education, Christianity, Islam, westernization, easternization, capitalism, and communications have been thrust —I was going to say 'almost suddenly.' Although these influences are inter-related, yet their effects upon the life of the African are confusing, and the African is in a very bad state."[6] Here is an African who looks anxiously in all directions, but especially backward.

Another African, a Ghanaian caught up in the throes of this decision, wrote the following poem:

> But whither bound,
> O Africa
> Oh, whitherbound?
>
> Backward?
> To days of drums

And festal dances in the shade
Of sun-kist palms;
Backward?
To untutored days
When maid was ever chaste
And lad abhorred unhallowed ways
For dread of ancient gods:
Backward?
To dark thatched huts
Where kindness reigned
And solace dwelt,
Backward to SUPERSTITION?

Or forward?
Forward! To what?
The slums, where man is dumped upon man;
Where penury
And misery
Have made their hapless homes,
And all is dark and drear?
Forward! To what?
The factory
To grind hard hours
In an inhuman mill,
In one long ceaseless spell?

Forward! To what?
To the reeking round
Of medieval crimes,
Where the greedy hawks
Of *Aryan stock*
Prey with bombs and guns
On men of *lesser breeds?*
Forward to CIVILIZATION?

—DEI ANANG, GHANA

Edwin Smith, the missionary-writer who tried as hard as anyone in his generation to help Christians see the good in tribalism, gives the following account:

The question was put to an old man in Nyasaland: "When you say, 'A
good town,' what is the sense of your words?" This was his answer:

"A good town is where the headman and the older people are respected by all, and where they, in their turn, give thought to all, even the children. It is only a good town where the young have respect for their fathers and mothers and all their relations, and where no person makes an attempt to do damage to another. If there is even one person who puts others in a bad light, or does damage to them, then the town is bad."[7]

In the same book he tells how, in a girls' school at Mbereshi, in Northern Rhodesia, one of the head girls went wrong and had to be shut out of the school. Miss Shaw, the head of the school, was very sad when she gave the news to the other "bakalamba" (girl-leaders) of how the girl had said: "Let me go away before my equals have knowledge of my shame, they will have a feeling of hate for me for damaging their good name." Mr. Smith continues the description:

There was bitter weeping among the girls, and they went to bed without a word. The day after, Miss Shaw saw that not one of them was taking her food, and when she put the question, Why? the answer was: "Our friend has to be shut out. We are conscious that it is not possible for her to go on living here with us, but our desire is to have a part in her punishment. She is one of us and we have all things in common with her—what is ours is hers, what is hers is ours, the good and the bad. We are taking our part in her shame." So they went without food for a time and gave up other pleasures. By their help the girl who had gone wrong got back the respect of the people and the forgiveness of her relations.[8]

Where else in the world does one find a better description of the therapeutic community, where breach of fellowship is acknowledged and where the community itself initiates the reconciliation by taking part in the blame and shame? The Christian doctrine of confession and restitution, on an open basis, is often seen in reality within the old tribal structure.

If the reader suspects that the virtues of tribalism are overdrawn, let him refer to the writings of Elspeth Huxley, the journalist who devotes most of her attention to Africa and who is not known as an uncritical friend of everything African. Writ-

ing in the *New York Times Magazine* ("Drums of Change Beat
for Africa's Tribes," Nov. 29, 1959, and "Africa's First Loyalty,"
Sept. 18, 1960), she affirmed: "Tribalism is like the big striped
umbrellas held over the chiefs who parade in ceremonies that
once involved the slaughter of slaves. Everyone can shelter there.
No tribesman is ever left alone. Every fellow-tribesman is bound
by sacred rules to give him shelter, food and comfort whenever
he needs it—a perfect welfare state, based on blood relationship." She elaborates to say: "There are no old maids. . . . Under
tribalism prostitution was unknown. . . . African society had no
prisons, either, and no police, in pre-colonial days. . . . In 'African
eyes, the death penalty is completely illogical, and so is life imprisonment. . . . Broken marriages under tribalism are very rare.
. . . Respect for old age is pretty well universal among African
tribesmen." She concludes:

> It would be a tragedy for Africa if tribalism were so to weaken as to
> leave the mass of people with no feeling of unity, of security, of be-
> longing to a group. It has inspired all of Africa's arts—its vigorous
> dances, its rich legends, the carvings, masks, decorative bead and basket
> work, songs and music. Despite its crudity, it is a spiritual force as
> well as a remarkably successful way of living in society and of han-
> dling family affairs. For his tribe a man will endure great hardships,
> even sacrifice his life. It is his guarantee of immortality. It gives him
> his mother-tongue and the pride that lifts him above the status of a
> rootless person. If tribalism is to go—and it will be a long time before
> this happens—the great need is for something better to put in its
> place: some true spiritual belief and stable social organization.

In the light of these expressions on the part of Africans about
tribalism, it appears that we cannot write off the present appeal
it makes to the African mind. "The perishing progeny of Ham"
—as the early missionaries referred to him—is not *perishing* so
fast. That "old things pass away and everything becomes new"
is to some extent true, but the new is confusing and questionable. It is a truism to say that the present-day African is the most
bewitched of modern men. His deep psychological longing as he
looks backward, and his gripping misgiving as he looks ahead,

we in the West must try to understand. The one-way passage
from tribalism to Christianity no longer operates. We know all
too well the story of the early missionaries tramping roughshod
over Africa, knocking loose the cultural ties and ridiculing the
treasured beliefs of the pagans. Of course they were part of an
intrusion that included commerce, colonial occupation, and communications. What they did may be explainable when we remember the missionary zeal couched in terms of the "saving
gospel" for "the poor lost heathen" and the prejudices he shared
in common with the Europeans of his day. But the radical up-
rooting of the African way of life, without a fair appraisal of its
inherent value and without a severe criticism of what is being
substituted in its place, must come to a stop. From every hand
comes the demand that, amid the cultural assaults on Africa
nowadays, the missionary must stand alongside him as a friend
to help reclaim and restore the good in the old and blend it with
the best in the new. Spiritual salvation does not occur in a social
vacuum.

The term which has been coined to express the self-respect of
the newly self-conscious African is "the African Personality" (in
French areas, *Négritude*). In politics, Kwame Nkrumah is the
spokesman for it; in literature, L.S. Senghor. The latter, writing
in the journal that features this point of view, *Le Monde Noir,*
raised the question as long ago as 1950 in an article entitled
*l'Afrique s'interroge: subir ou choisir?: "*At the crossroads, the
African soul asks itself: to submit or to choose? . . . Ought we to
go forward? Ought we to go back? There is the dilemma, and
our anguish is heart-rending. What a sad situation is ours. We
had faith in the West and now the West commits suicide. However, we are obstinate and believe that man can become better
again. . . . Far from resigning himself to become a servile copy of
an alien model, the African ought to separate the traits of an
original culture and be ready to reunite in a new way of life and
thought what he himself possesses of the best with carefully
selected gifts from the West."[9]

More and more this critical reappraisal of westernization is trickling down to the masses of Africans. There is the story of the chief visiting England who finally turned upon his detractors: "You think that *better off* means *better!*" The Nigerian author, Ojike, phrased the difference this way: "The West is a paper and machine culture; Africa is a land and man culture."[10]

If, as A. N. Whitehead has written, civilization can be characterized by Truth, Beauty, Adventure, Art, and Peace, then much can be made for the case that Africans have contributed a great deal to civilization. Take Peace, for instance. It is hard for the westerner to realize that African tribal society has an ordered existence equal to human society anywhere on earth, and that the intertribal wars were seldom as devastating as the mechanized mass extermination of modern warfare. The African is quick to notice this. The West Nigerian Prime Minister wrote in his book, "The least enlightened Nigerian knows that the fiercest of our intertribal wars did not compare either in ruthlessness or carnage with what are called 'patrol clashes' in civilized warfare."[11] The distinguished Ghanaian sociologist, Dr. Kofi A. Busia, describes his reaction as follows: "In the year 1945 an Ashanti, namely myself, was browsing round a bookshop in Oxford. I picked up a book of photographs . . . of some of the concentration camps of Europe. I saw photographs of caves where human bones were piled up and where human bodies were reduced to ashes. . . . I cut out one of these pages and pasted it in my book of descriptions of the Gold Coast in 1817. Opposite the very big picture of a barbarian chief in all his glory I put one of these photos from a European concentration camp. Beneath the one I wrote 'Ashanti 1817' and beneath the other 'Europe 1945,' with no no other comment."[12]

In Art, the astute African observers traveling in America have called attention to the preponderance of military statues in our public squares. Certainly it is in art that Africans have made a decisive contribution. Ladislas Segy, whose galleries and writings in America have won for African art a place alongside the best in the world, declares, "The fact that African art stood on such a very high level of artistic creation leads us to ascertain that only a well-intergrated culture, only a communally felt and accepted ideology, could have produced such a high quality of art. . . . We had to reject the tendentious reports that Africans were 'savage' people. We trusted the validity of African sculptures as their documents and we insisted that savage people could not have produced such magnificent art."[13] The famous modern sculptor, Epstein, kept his home and workshop filled with African art that it might inspire him. African sculpture, he said, "is supposed to be rude, savage, the product of uncultured and uncivilized people. I find, on the contrary, restraint in craftsmanship, delicacy, and sensitiveness, a regard for the material, and none of the stupid vulgarity, pomposity, and crudeness so evident in sculpture today."[14]

From these brief comments on African peace and art, we could enlarge upon their "democracy by discussion," their reverence for the land, their closely knit and sacred human relations. They have their weaknesses, as we all have heard, but the false notion that tribalism is no respectable culture is on the way to being rectified. A Belgian official in the Congo finally faced up to the change: "We used to think the African's mind was an empty vessel, and that all we had to do was to pour European civilization into it. No one would dare now make such a statement, but our policies are still based on that idea. We must rethink everything." With the Mau Mau atrocities in Kenya and the confusion of the Congolese, there is apparently a campaign on the part of Afro-phobes to resurrect the myth of wholesale African barbarism. The wise will look upon these rare occurrences as social phenomena with as complicated a background as the concentration camps of Germany or the lynchings of Dixie. Living in a world in which all make their contribution to human destiny, we cannot afford to take the worst estimate of tribalism.

Islam

● ● ● ● ● ● ● ● ● ●

The greatest surprise for the visitor who covers all Africa is the activity and extensiveness of Islam. Without going into figures, it is possible to declare that Islam is the religion of Africa, if one takes this to mean the religion which unifies more people under a common worship and a common ethic. This holds not merely for North Africa but for the belt of the continent as well, where if twenty-five countries gained their freedom today, twenty of them would tomorrow undoubtedly be Moslem-dominated, on the basis of universal suffrage and bloc-voting. Christianity is, in spite of its influence, a minority religion, almost an alien religion. Tribalism is a religious attitude divided into a thousand incompatible forms and already given the deathblow. Nationalism itself is in danger of being subordinated to the political maneuvering of a renascent Islam.

What is more surprising, this new power of Islam has come about to the confounding of the experts. At the beginning of this century the historians of religion were announcing that Islam in Africa South "is finished." As late as the mid-century a writer in the newly founded *Ecumenical Review* affirmed, "Islam is moribund." Nothing of the sort has resulted. Billy Graham's recent sally into Africa confronted a militant faith: they challenged him to open debate, to test cases, and actually barred his entrance into certain countries. To his dismay he discovered that Christian evangelism is at a standstill (not able to match the rise in population), and that, on the contrary, for every African won to Christ, seven are being won to Allah (however, this last figure was not arrived at by an actual poll).

No question about it, the religion which historically has been the most powerful opponent of Christianity in the contest for Africa is on the offensive. Young Moslems, newly acquainted with the centers in Cairo and Khartoum and intoxicated by the pan-Arabic, pan-Moslem dream, are busily demanding that Arabic, the language of the Koran, be taught in public schools. They urge the enforcement of a modified Sharia law, and propagate the principle of a theocratic state. Moreover, missionaries from faraway Pakistan comprise the necessary outside stimulus. All the way around Africa is this the case. Radio and newspaper have substituted for the sword and the steed. Schools and liberalized mosques are recruiting centers in the stead of the patriarchal fiat. More and more youth are willing to admit to their faith, so that on university campuses they are defending their beliefs and demanding equal representation in the curriculum and chapel life. Even politicians are obliged to cater to their practices and leaders.

The presence of the Moslem in Africa is not restricted to a few areas but is widely scattered. As far down as Capetown there are 65,000 Moslems. The number in that city has increased phenominally, having grown from the twenty-five thousand that faced the famous preacher to the Moslems, Dr. Samuel Zwemer, when he made his appeal there in the twenties. Upon inquiring about this rise, I learned that they are a close-knit social unit. Industrious, sober, and skilled workmen, they have hewn for themselves a niche higher in the social wall than any other of the non-European groups. When they intermarry, they insist invariably that the marriage partner entering their culture become a Moslem. Nonetheless, Egyptian money helped finance the erection of a mosque on this toe of Africa. Also in Durban the massive blue stucco mosque overshadows the main street of the downtown area.

Elsewhere, as in Uganda, Kenya, and Tanganyika, one is never without a reminder of Islam. The fez is everywhere and every village has its mosque, if no more than a bamboo enclosure or lines marked in the dusty square. They have status, too. At certain seasons, the East African airways are crowded with heavy-bundled pilgrims on their way to Mecca, to return as local heroes. A young African prized becoming an Alhajj more than owning a house. Asked why, his reply was, "Because the former is having a house after this life, which is a better house than one built in this world." The Secretary General of the Uganda National Congress is a Moslem. Tanganyika has its All-African Moslem Union.

But the flood tide flows all through central and west Africa as well, down to the coast. Nearly every town, even in the southern coastal area, has its Moslem community; the "Zongos" are everywhere. Anyone wishing to meet Moslems has not to go far. The Hausa tribesmen, like the Swahili on the east, are the aggressive traders who have pushed down the giant rivers with their multiple backwaters into virtually every tribal village. Nowadays the Ahmadiyya sect is using the radio, the press, and the school to present "the Faith." It was the professional of this sect who challenged Billy Graham both in Nigeria and in Kenya. The mayor of Freetown is Moslem, and Moslem students at historic Fourah Bay College collected money and cement to construct a mosque in 1960. The only training college for African Moslems in East Africa opened in 1954, with a Sudanese principal.

Typical of the new self-consciousness is the mood in Nigeria. At the university, Moslem students are pressing for a mosque, demanding proportionate funds as did the Catholics and the Protestants for their respective chapels. While there is no Moslem faculty, pressure is demanding their appointment. Not half the students are Moslem (due to the scarcity of their secondary schools and to the northern suspicion of the southern institution), but recently under the "back-to-land" movement, Moslem students openly admitted their allegiance.

The levels of the African Moslems fall into three: First, there are the aggressive "theologians," who take the lead in the professional missionary and teaching work. Second, there are the vast numbers who do not know why they are a member of the Faith. Third, there is what is called a "floating middle," those who belong to the uprooted new proletariat—urbanized, industrial-ized, and partly educated—and who are still seeking their bear-ings. They are the ones who support the following movements.

On the night of September 23, 1959, the city hall of Durban was packed with people who had come to celebrate the birth-day of Mohammed. Even the mayor graced the gathering. (In this east coast city, Indians number 110,000, but only 15 per cent of them are Moslems.) The crowd came to hear the Prophet eulogized and reasons given why Islam is winning over Christian-ity. The speaker was a leader of the Universal Truth Movement, which is translating the Koran into African languages. His argu-ments were forthright and logical—presented as some Christians list their contribution to progress in the West: (1) Christianity has failed and Islam has succeeded because Mohammed's fol-lowers believe in world brotherhood. "For instance, Arabia was within a stone's throw of Jerusalem; yet for 600 years the reli-gion that preaches 'love thy neighbor' did not love its nearest neighbor. Moreover, after the Prophet came the Christians loved even less, turning against the Moslems for another 600 years with the sword of the Crusades. Since that period we have had noth-ing but accusations against us from western Christian writers."

(2) The Prophet freed mankind from race oppression, teaching that the Arabs had no superiority over other people. In his last sermon he insisted that there be no oppression. "Of all religions, only Islam practices brotherhood, believes in the family of man." The speaker went on to explain that "though it was foreign to the Arab to accept the African as equal, the Prophet forced the Egyptian king to accept a Moslem deputation including an Abys-sinian, though the king felt that all Abyssinians were 'meant to be slaves.'" He concluded that today "we have no color bar; certainly we do not believe as the main church of South Africa, which teaches that some men are to be slaves of other men."

(3) The Prophet lifted the status of women the world over. "He looked to the East, he looked to the West, and found woman oppressed. In India she was burned on her husband's pyre; in England she did not get political freedom until the '30s, and

even today she is obliged to take her husband's name." (The speaker apparently failed to notice that there was not one woman in the city hall.)

(4) The Prophet anticipated moon travel when he said, "Go as far as you wish into the spaces of the stars and the moon, and you will find the glory and majesty of God." The speaker said he thought the Prophet would have encouraged space travel. This was timely preaching since the Russians had launched their moon rocket only a few days before.

Far on the west coast, in Lagos, Nigeria, the *Daily Times* was running a full-page feature entitled "Calling All Moslems." Nigeria, which gained its independence in 1960, has a strong Moslem majority in its northern province, the population of which exceeds that of the other two provinces. On October 16, 1959, the *Times* column dealt with human brotherhood, "a Moslem ideal": "There is no gainsaying the fact that of all the divine messengers, founders and builders of the different creeds, faiths and religious systems who at any time, in any land and in any form contributed to the social uplift and moral and spiritual regeneration of humanity, the share of Mohammed, the Teacher of Islam, was by far the greatest. And one of the greatest services to mankind of this noblest of men was his clear and unequivocal condemnation of, and the effective measures he took to abolish, those social injustices which were in world-wide practice in his days." The writer describes how slavery was practiced in the Roman and Persian empires, among Jews and Christians as well as Arabs. But, he continues, the Prophet took a stern stand against both slavery and the color bar. "If he could, he would abolish by a stroke of the pen a system so repugnant and revolting, so destructive of all the noble human instincts."

The foregoing sampling does not mean that Islam in Africa is all of one piece. The most reliable commentators hold that much of the continent is still in the grip of medieval Islam and has not modernized its appeal. Many Africans cannot forget the part Arabs played in the slave raids. But the newly self-conscious Moslems are on their toes, and eager to capture Africa in this transitional period. They see the vacuum being created by the withdrawal of western colonialism, and they are well aware that Christianity stands to suffer the most by this hasty retreat. They are not above seizing the political ascendancy. Few people can forget that it is the first premier of independent Nigeria who shouted heatedly on the floor of the Legislative Council as long ago as 1947: "We do want independence and we shall demand it when the time is ripe and we shall even be prepared to fight for it if necessary . . . but I should like to make it clear to you that if the British quitted Nigeria now at this stage the Northern people would continue their interrupted march to the sea."[1] John Scott, an American specialist on Africa, has summarized four possible results of Islamic penetration: First, Islam is a vehicle for Egyptian expansionist aspirations in Black Africa. Second, as in Nigeria, it may lead to a schism. Third, it may make multi-party parliamentary democracy all but unworkable. Fourth, it may open the way for Soviet influence.[2]

Nor is this Moslem aggression unwelcomed by the nationalists fighting for African status. For years the burden of the independence movement was borne by nations mainly Moslem: Egypt, Sudan, Libya, Tunis, Morocco. Indigenous nationalism finds in Islam its most effective ally against the presence of Europeans, of western United Nations, and of western commercial interests. It is said locally that "the unity of the Moslems and the orthodoxy of the Koran are marching side by side with the progressive independence of the colored peoples vis-à-vis the Europeans." Moreover, Islam promotes Pan-Africanism since it is one of the few factors that unite the African nationalists of the former British and French colonies. Further, it is reported that the United Arab Republic is planning to add "religious attachés" to its diplomatic posts in Africa.

All too soon, westerners may find themselves confronting a unified culture more hostile to their overtures than they ever found under tribal conditions. Some observers have already reminded us that the highly insulated Arabicized and Koranic African culture is far more strange and resistant than the many versions of the African folk culture. It is clear that the Moslem world furnishes a way of life foreign to the westerner. It may even be said that the westerner finds himself more at home with the "jungle" African than with the "desert" Arab (although there have been notable exceptions, such as the romantic Lawrence of Arabia). Certainly for the purposes of the missionary there was more to lend itself to ready adjustment in the African tribal society.

Charges that Islam is a socio-political system more than a religion can best be made by westerners prepared to separate their own Christianity from the strait jacket of Europeanization. Nowhere is this strait jacket more obvious than in Africa. It can be said that the European finds himself much more at home among the awakening, transitional Black African than among the long-established Arabic African. Can this be because he finds it easier to "lord it over" the black man, having assumed that the latter has no culture and history worth preserving? On the contrary, westerners have found the Moslem culture a formidable citadel. Their relations continue to be marred by the depreciatory epithets some of them have hurled at Moslems and by the series of unholy wars designed to decimate the Moslems. Perhaps the ugliest page of Christian history is Christendom's record of relationships with the Moslems. This, too, is an unavoidable part of the present-day Islam-Christian confrontation in Africa.

However, it is vital that the West not fall into the "fear Islam, hate Islam" complex. The so-called "Moslem threat" is not altogether an evil; its complex nature makes for a mixed blessing. Africans themselves do not regard Islam with the same fright that seizes some westerners. Sir Francis Ibiam, the Nigerian medical doctor who is lay chairman of the All-Africa Church Conference, expressed dismay that many missionaries were upset over the rising Moslem tide. "Leave us alone," he has cautioned. "We have a history of good relations here in Nigeria, which ought not be tampered with by outsiders intruding upon us with their studies and conferences." He feels that Christians and Moslems get along more amicably in Africa than they do anywhere else in the world, and that his countrymen would do well to preserve this good relationship in which several religions vie on an open field. But whether the Moslems will continue to appreciate pluralism in religion when they secure for themselves the upper hand is another question.

Perhaps there is a hint as to the answer to this question in the history of Islam in modern Black Africa. There seem to be three stages. First, there was the colonial occupational policy which in some quarters tended to favor the extension of Islam by not encouraging, if not outrightly forbidding, Christian missions to enter designated Moslem territories. Consequently, European occupation, by entrusting Moslem natives with trading, military, and governmental administrative posts, gave superior prestige to the Faith. Second, there followed the stage of agitation for independence, where nationalism—especially where Moslems formed a sizable bloc of the population—incorporated Moslem favoritism. This is noticeable at the moment in such countries as Sudan, Guinea, and Somaliland, where Christian missionaries are being expelled or finding it hard to secure visas. In my talks with missionary leaders in Uganda, they were apprehensive that a similar development would occur there. In fact, as has been suggested, this mood may sweep Africa during the decade of nationalization. But there promises to be a third stage—one such as Egypt seems to be entering at present. A more open and tolerant mood prevails once the nation becomes more secure and accepts the principle of cultural pluralism. This last stage may prove small hope for Christians who, in their favored position as a minority force under an alien power, exercised considerable privileges in the past. All that can be said for such nostalgic Christians is that they must come back to earth, to the reality of the present. It may be that in this new climate the Christian faith will present itself more persuasively. I was told by Christians working in Cairo that since Nasser, conditions have been "more favorable." They seem to think that "Islam governments can accept the principle that different religions may exist within the same state in a new way, no longer as tolerated minorities, but as equals with the same rights and obligations." The secularization which

has occurred to a large extent in the Mediteranean Islamic countries may be the direction of all Africa. If so, then Christianity
and Islam may find themselves handmaidens in the larger fight
against the complete secularization of life.

A further consideration should steer the West from the course
of anti-Islam feeling. This pertains to the highly debatable thesis
that Islam constitutes an intermediate position between African
tribal religion and the refinement of Christianity. As tribalism
with its animism breaks down, Islam offers the whole gamut of
transition before the spiritualization of higher religion. It therefore tends to reduce the opposition to a minimum through its
series of gradations. Islam provides a gradual penetration. It can
be argued, without necessarily supporting the above thesis, that
Islam does offer an easier transition for the African moving from
his own cultural background to something new. The degree of
accommodation, the social step, is much shorter from tribalism to
Islam than it is from tribalism to Protestant Christianity. To
put this in words expressed by an African, "There are two good
roads leading to heaven: the Christian religion, which is very
complicated and too strict, all right for white people who are
better educated than we are, and the religion of Mohammed,
which is simpler and better suited to the colored people."

Christians who admit the similarities in beliefs and the common historical rootage of the two faiths are more likely not to
be disturbed by the trend toward Islam among the Africans.
They would claim that this is preparatory to the evangelization
of the African. Conversion is progressive, and getting the African
to become a Moslem is one step on the way. Christianity will
eventually profit by Islam's being the intermediate stage before
its own adoption. On the other hand, those Christians who are
acquainted with the intransigence of the Moslem in the face of
the Christian appeal, not budging one inch from his stand nor
surrendering an iota of his beliefs, are thoroughly skeptical of
this thesis. Typical, they say, of the absolutely unyielding and
incredibly polite resistance toward Christianity are the patients
from the Maure and Wolof tribes at St. Louis-du-Senegal where

the Sisters of St. Joseph de Cluny have ministered for almost a century. When they return home they invariably say: "God is good; the Sisters are good"—and they proceed to the mosque to thank Allah for giving them these good Sisters, but not a single one has moved an inch toward Christianity.

Moreover, there are missionaries who maintain that the fatalism, the collectivism, and the exclusiveness of Islam are much more unfortunate for the African than is his native state. One such contender declared, "In every case the African who has become a Moslem is much farther away from the God of Jesus Christ than when he was a pagan." In French territory it is sometimes said that Islam "est le grand frere du fetichisme." Still the key to the whole question remains: what is best for the Africans?

Let us turn now to reasons why Islam is presently so active and so extensive in Africa. Ignoring the fact of the innate attractiveness and solid unity of Islam as a theological system, we concentrate on the social, political, and moral grounds for its expansion. First, the Moslem is not alien to Africa. Too much cannot be made of the fact that the Moslem proselytizer comes as one African to another. Mohammed is reported to have visited Africa, and his faith was in part born on African soil. In the twentieth century, Islam claims major numbers in Africa, and, as was said, Africa can indeed be referred to as a Moslem continent. But, above all, there is no color bar. The black man is not far from believing that Christianity is the religion of whites. Where the Moslem is one of them—eating, sleeping, and making merry with them—the European, even the missionary in most cases, is isolated in his compound, eating by himself, obviously enjoying his own brand of entertainment, with his eye on "home." The westerner remains detached, at a distance, about as *related* as the fly-by-night American salesman. Where the Moslem enters into local life, is at the center, the very appearance of a European at a village dance may dampen the spirit, if not kill the affair. The Moslem mixes readily with the villagers; they are nearly on the same standard of living; they easily adapt their religious formalities to local customs. Some missionaries may reside near villages for years, even decades, without so much as a courtesy call upon the local chief, while the Moslem is at the center of life, at the marketplace and the festivals. The African himself will tell you how much this impresses them. "You know how much importance we place upon the meal. The feast is the place of brotherhood, of happiness, of plans." Above all, the Moslem intermarries. The white man may take liberties, may even possess a secret concubine or a second wife (his squaw), but there is almost no case of a European male married on western legal and social basis to an African woman in the whole of the continent. It is therefore not strange that Islam comes to be known as "the religion of the blacks." It is closer to the African in color, culture, and class. It is a visible brotherhood, not a church beyond the seas.

A second major factor is the total social unity which the Moslem preserves among the African. There is not the break with the culture which accompanies Christianity's introduction, where the African is left in the lurch. The Moslem leaves his convert still rooted in his indigenous way of life. The religious organization of Islam where there is no distinction between clergy and laity, and little between politics and religion, fits into the African mold. Contrary to what they observe of the Europeans living in their midst, and of what the European does in his home countries, Africans observe that Moslem religion and daily life are of one piece. Particularly is this true of the daily externals of the Faith and the extensive and powerful influence of Sharia law and custom. The five concrete acts of the faithful, so rigidly observed and so colorful, move the onlooker. The Ramadan fans the entire village for a whole month. Then there is the elementary but effective educational method of the Koranic schools. The African readily learns by rote, and when taught knows great portions of the Koran by heart—sometimes without knowing the meaning of a single word. I was told by a missionary in Nyasaland that little children playing in earshot of the teaching grounds would sing Arabic phrases. Moreover, the very foreignness of the tongue attracts the African. Islamic names appeal to Nigerians, for instance, as much as do Jewish names appeal to westerners. At a public gathering in Nigeria where prayers were offered, a Christian prayed in Yoruba, a Moslem in Arabic. One of those present reported that the prayer in Arabic seemed to appeal more to the worshipers than the one in their own mother tongue. In addition, it is not trivial to point out that Arabic does not have the odium which English has acquired as the language of the conquerors and of *baaskap*.

Thus Islam spreads by its pervasive attractiveness and adjustibility. For instance, most of its celebrations take place in the home, not in the mosque. They become an affair for the neighboring people, who are attracted by the beauty, color, music, dancing, and simplicity which characterize the celebrations. People who come to witness are softened for the Faith. Where Christianity originates "across the sea" and insists upon its new institutions, its new taboos, and its abstract ideas, Islam is ever present in its closeness, both in geography and in psychology. The African is not far from believing that Christianity is not the religion of Christians at all, but, as it were, a form of worship without believers, professed by a caste of clerics; worthy no doubt, but ultimately beyond his understanding . . . hence he becomes a Moslem.

Third, the Moslem faith was not introduced "artificially" but came, shall we say, more naturally, by the impenetration of the northern trader. The long outdated and questionable label, "the religion of the sword," can in Africa be replaced more accurately by "the religion of the trader." The Arab has ever carried Islam with him on his long commercial trips which he undertakes south of the Sahara and around the coasts. Each Moslem is an evangelist in the street, in the public places, on the road. A local commentator reports, "He teaches Islam to his fellow merchants at the same time that he breaks the cola nut" (a West African token of hospitality as prevalent as "the pause that refreshes" in America). The Arabic trader, and his Moslem African counterpart, is indeed a pervasive and insistent person. He can be found pressing his bargain almost everywhere in Africa. His white flowing robes and his fez are in every village. An instance of the fact of his ubiquity is the series of paintings which Oxford University Press published on the occasion of Nigeria's independence, where in virtually all of them the Moslem trader is depicted at the center of the bustling village life. We may contrast this lay witness of Islam with the professional clericalism with which we have propagated our faith there and have foisted it upon African Christians.

But it would be unfair to claim for the trader's informal presentation of the Faith the main weight of Moslem success. Two other forces are of equal influence. One of these has been the wide use of Moslem troops in the colonial military campaigns and maneuvers in Africa. The British found them able, and to this day the Ghana military police wear the fez. In French territory every man is dressed in a Moslem uniform and badge. The continued unfolding of this drama is apparent in the United Nations forces occupying the Congo in the summer of 1960, where the Moslem Tunisian troops predominated. The paradox of the past is that the very Europeanization of Africa promoted the spread of Islam.

The other force which accelerated Moslem evangelism was the mass-impulse led by a few chiefs which occurred in some parts of Africa. Wholesale tribal conversion was not unknown to Christian missions, and the Moslems have relied more upon it, especially since European penetration. The report from Senegal mentions that the Grand Serigne des Mourides travels about in a luxurious car with liveried chauffeur, using the telephone, having his own private chapel as well as his own secluded harem, and who, having close official contacts with the authorities of the country, makes a good business out of his faithful followers.

That Islam is learning the techniques of western propaganda is manifest in the way they utilize mass media—the radio and press. The Ahmadiyya sect, with its liberalized version of the Faith, has launched a major campaign all over Africa South. Money and missionaries come from as far away as Pakistan.

Fourth, the cultural affinity between the African societies and the Moslems has unquestionably benefited the latter. The traditional social structure of tribalism, where collective life swallows the individual, lends itself to the social grouping of Islam. As has been repeatedly observed, Africa's religious and social life cannot be considered apart; they are one. Accordingly, J. S. Trimingham concludes that "one of the primary reasons for its [Islam's] progress is that it has become an African religion whose agents are African, which can be assimilated gradually without causing too great disruption in communal life."[3] Since Islam offers all stages of transition in its considerable degree of accommodation to African ways, the social step is much shorter from tribalism to Islam than it is from tribalism to Christianity. Christianity, with its radical self-affirmation, its abstract verbal symbols, and its western dress, demands a cultural revolution almost too great for the ordinary African. (This is not to say that many do not make the switch; they do, some so well that by imitation they excel their teachers!) All this is not to imply that conversion to Islam is merely an easy exchange of false gods. Those persons ridiculing Islam see it as little more than a new animism, an empty formalism, and only a slightly less degrading culture with its backward role for women and its low-level education. It is true that Black Africa Islam tends to be of a lower sort than the Mediterranean and Asian varieties. Nonetheless, Islam can be credited with introducing the African to a wider family and world loyalty, reinforcing such private virtues as teetotalism and honesty, and bringing a uniform law code. As the liberalized version of Islam takes hold among the educated and urban African, it may be expected to strengthen education and democratic processes.

Fifth, we may conclude that some of Africa's current response to Islam is due to the rising anti-western attitude and the feeling that Africa must get its religion as well as its moral and material strength from Afro-Asian sources. Islam is part of the package that comes with Nasser's wooing, with university education outside the West, and with economic and military aid from the

Arabic powers. Already Arab bankers are busy establishing the first noncolonial banking structure in West Africa. Its president predicted in 1960, "Africans will have confidence in us, because the Arabs in many cases share a common religion and because many Arabs are members of the African community." A new social union is appearing on the surface of the globe. (Islam as the carrier of Black racism is a phenomenon more outside than inside Africa.)

Sixth, not least among the reasons for the African going Moslem is the failure of the Church itself—the mistakes she made in her own presentation. Accordingly, we need not look altogether in astonishment at the Moslem success, but to the very shortcomings of the western Church. Reduced to a humbler mood, Christians may indeed now wonder if the Africans are not right to reject a Christianity identified as it is with western materialism and white supremacy. The amazing fact is that so many Africans have become Christians in spite of it all. Western Christians should be prodded to re-examine their approach, especially when it is observed that the Moslems effected their triumph without benefit of hospitals and schools.

In the light of the bright new sun of Islam shining in Africa, it is not surprising that Christians are obliged to take a new approach. For a long time they have taken the traditional tack of education, medicine, and evangelism. But, as we have noted, neither the indirect approach of the first two nor the direct approach of the latter has been adequate in the face of Islam. Consequently, direct evangelism of African Moslems has been virtually forsaken from Cairo to Capetown. Few missionaries can now be found who make the frontal attack. In all the vast area I covered I was unable to find anyone dedicated specifically to conversations with Black African Moslems. There must be some—perhaps many; but the fact that they are so obscure helps explain the misunderstanding, the enigma, and the impasse in relationships.

In South Africa, I was referred by the Dutch Reformed Church to a dominie who was supposed to be an expert on the problem. He knew Arabic and had been a missionary among the Cape

Malays for some twenty years, but from the outset of the interview he was a disappointment. He knew little of current happenings, nor had he kept up his contacts. He confessed that in all his years among them he had known of but two converts. Both of them were results of extraneous circumstances, rather than being creditable to spiritual reasons. "They are hard to reach," he admitted. "In the daytime they work hard. As soon as they return home they are about their prayers, three in succession. And one dare not enter their homes and approach their women. They are virtually inaccessible—inaccessible both physically and mentally. I do not mean that you cannot make friends among them. You can, and I had many. But the minute you broach the subject of a Saviour, they shy away, likely never to give you a second chance."

But, as was said, there are signs that this older approach of simply putting one form of ecclesiolatry or bibliolatry over against another is being abandoned. Experiments now being tried are in terms of on-the-level conferences, where each gingerly feels out the other in the bilateral summit-conference fashion. Within recent years several such meetings have boded well for the future. In the spring of 1959 in Asmara, Ethopia, a conference of eighty-three delegates from thirty-two church bodies met to consider relations with Islam and to issue a message outlining this new approach. Sponsored largely by the Commission on Ecumenical Relations (United Presbyterian Church of the U.S.A.), the conference was the brain child of Dr. Ben Reed of the United States. In a similar mood, the World Student Christian Federation called a "conversational" conference in North Africa for the fall of 1959. In projecting this, they prepared the climate with an issue of *The Student World* (Second Quarter, 1959) devoted to the subject, "Confrontation with Islam in Africa." There they honestly faced "the new birth which Islam is experiencing" and confessed that "one can hardly speak of a confrontation as having ever taken place anytime, anywhere." These are mere beginnings. In 1960 the University

Divinity School of Ghana for the first time invited Moslems to their Easter convocation.

Islam in Africa simply illustrates on a broad canvas and in brilliant colors the ideological competition for the minds of that awakening nation. Easy assumptions about the adoption of western standards, including the Christian religion, are no longer justifiable. What the African needs for his own self-development is subject to radical review. Whether the three parties involved —Islam, Christianity, and the African himself—are mature enough to meet each other on neutral ground to thrash out the future direction of their respective contributions to each other's fullest development and usefulness is highly doubtful.

Christianity

3

●　●　●　●　●　●　●　●　●　●

During the devastating Leopoldville riots of 1959, on that fateful Sunday when the rioters marched en masse up Prince Baudoin Street destroying everything "European" until they were barricaded just short of the new city uptown, a young American missionary couple were returning from an outpost mission station. By a stroke of Providence, an African detoured them from their usual route via Prince Baudoin—where their car would surely have suffered the fate of all the other overturned, burned motorcars—and they reached their home in the African settlement safely, completely unaware of the outbreak. That night they slept soundly, they and their four children. But they were among the few missionaries who did, because all the others had scampered for shelter. On the following day, when the Belgians allowed the police to kill several hundred in retaliation (although not one white was killed) they felt the reaction. As night drew on, their fear increased, for the Africans, formerly their neighbors and friends, milled menacingly. They gathered their children about them and huddled together upstairs in frozen fright. "How long can we hold out? How long before they attack us?" was all they could think. In the midst of their apprehension they chanced to recall a similar riot in the history of Pearl Buck. As they remembered the story, Mrs. Buck's mother, sensing the mood of the rioters, had baked cookies all day and kept the pot boiling, ready to serve tea when and if they came. They did approach in their boisterous, destructive mood, but the mother met them at the open door and welcomed them. "Come in, please,"

49

she invited, "I have been expecting you all day and have some tea ready."

Even so the Congo missionaries decided to kneel in prayer in the besieged upper room, and they asked God to protect them as they attempted to repeat the kindness. They immediately switched on all the lights in the house, put the pot on, opened the front door, and even though it was late at night acted as if they were about their usual routine. And nothing happened. Since that day, they have remained in the suburb called *Cité Matet* where tens of thousands of Africans live. Their escape can surely be credited to the kind of continuous "open house" they have always kept for Africans.

The night I stayed with them there were nine adults for supper; the overworked mother had already sent the children to bed. As we ate, several other Africans dropped in. After supper we walked over to the African market, which resembled a cloud of fireflies with each tiny stall of squatting women lit by a candle. Then returning home we outcompeted the blaring noises of the bar-and-dance across the street with our group-singing of Stephen Foster favorites. The eyes of the Africans gleamed as we sang "The Old Folks at Home," and "Gone Are the Days." They were tasting a little bit of American openness and genuine Christian acceptance. And it was too good to be true.

What a different atmosphere prevailed in this missionary home in the middle of danger than prevailed in the plush European section to which the others had fled. The untold story concerns those Africans who risked their lives to protect whites during that terrible weekend that surprised Leopoldville. What they did can surely have arisen not alone from their generous human impulses but also in repayment for the kind of on-the-level relationships built by missionaries like these. They are the kind of missionary which may yet save the day for missions and the Church in the new Africa, if Christianity is to be saved.

For we must admit that hostile forces operate in the new Africa. There was a generation which thought the missionary could do no wrong. A younger African leader explained to me that his father belonged to that school, "But I just can't understand it." Recipient of mission benefits, he no longer belongs to the uncritical generation. "Missionaries, no! Christians, yes," is the way another African Christian leader phrased the present attitude. He defined the missionary as one who feels superior and acts condescendingly. Only the Christian, one who comes to another culture humble, admitting the limitations of his own background and seeing the merit in the new, and who is willing to listen to and be under the supervision of a national, if need be, is welcome.

It is surprising how much of the older attitude—of the one-way mission to "the heathen in his blindness"—still prevails among Christian missionaries in Africa, perhaps more than anywhere else in the world. All this is in spite of the revised training, including anthropology, given by some of the mission boards. The following poem depicting this attitude appeared in an American missionary journal in 1960:

> The heathen now is calling me,
> Hark, hark, I hear his voice;
> A land more dense for work I see,
> That work is now my choice.
> Would you say, "Stay!" when God said, "Go
> To that dark foreign land!"
> To spread the light, would you say, "No,"
> That bright their souls might stand?
> Those souls bowed down to wood and stone,
> They think their way is right;
> And when from earth their souls are gone
> To hell they take their flight.

Devolution (mission policy of letting the leadership fall into the hands of nationals) moves slowly. As late as the moment of the Congo crisis of 1960 few mission boards allowed Africans to head their missions, to control the committee votes, or to administer finances. Of the many Christian councils over Africa, few were manned by Africans. The turning over of all property and administration into the hands of an independent national unit of the international denomination was infrequent. And the ratio of the new type of missionary—trained in comparative anthropology and supplementing his evangelism with technical skills, willing to take a back seat in decision-making and to work under a national—to the old prototype was decreasing rather than improving, as the sectarians, mostly from America, steadily increased their numbers in Africa. The tragedy of mission work in Africa is, therefore, that just as the older mission boards which introduced Christianity into Africa awakened to the needs of the new day, they were suddenly overrun by sectarians who still operate under a nineteenth-century conception of missions. Usually sectarians are the "soul-saving" variety rather than the culture-appreciating; they believe only in enough education to read the Bible (they distrust higher education in their own life back home); they are politically irresponsible and racially segregated back home; and they are so sectarian as to believe that they alone have the whole truth and are consequently unable to co-operate with other Christian bodies. To these the Africans refer when they speak of "the white bulls fighting on the fair soil of Africa."

To repeat, the tragedy is that, just at the moment Christianity is awakening to the total culture challenge of new Africa, more and more mission stations are being financed and manned by sectarians, mostly from America, as the traditional Protestant churches from Europe and America recede for lack of funds and personnel. It seems that Africa is destined to come under the most conservative wing of Christianity, which is pietistic and individualistic, in which the salvation of souls is divorced from cultural values. This bodes ill for the full message of Christianity for Africa and the full ministry of the Church in new Africa. Edmund Ilogu, the well-traveled author who is now head of the religious programing of the Nigerian Broadcasting Company, referred to this as "the tyranny of the sectarians, with their loads of American money."

Signs of this reaction are already too obvious in the attitude of Christians toward politics, toward education, and toward literature. Regarding the last, it is no accident that the four most widely circulated magazines in all of Afrique Noire, besides the secular *Drum,* are Protestant: *African Challenge, Our Africa, Africa's Hope,* and *Envol.* They are African-oriented, have an attractive, eye-catching make-up, and sell on the newsstand. They lean toward the fundamentalist, pietistic point of view, and while nondenominational they are not positively ecumenical nor representative of the best biblical scholarship. What they accomplish is good, but leaves much to be desired.

The same is true for the short-wave radio stations. They are in the hands of American sectarians except for the new East Africa station manned by Lutherans. And as television opened in Africa for the first time, in 1959 in Nigeria, it promises little improvement.

Englishman Max Warren, probably along with the American Emory Ross the most authoritive person on Protestant work in Africa, feels that in Africa a rising nationalism has not yet decided to identify the Christian religion with European imperialism, and to reject both at the same time. He thinks the die is not yet cast. But "the revolt against things western" is bringing the Church into criticism. And the African who for so long never said anything but "yes" to the missionary is now saying "no." The missionary who unavoidably remained an alien is regarded as one who looks with disdain from his carefully preserved compound pedestal and who refuses to make concessions to the local adaptation of the faith. And the new Africa is finding abundant evidence of the joint invasion of "the mercenary, the military, and the missionary." Did not the most renowned of the African missionaries, David Livingstone, establish that unholy trilogy upon the occasion of his triumphal appeal to the Cambridge University audience of 1857 when he begged for "brave young men who would open up Africa for commerce and missions"? He concluded, "I go back to Africa to try to make an open path for commerce and Christianity; do you carry out the work which I have begun. I leave it with you."

In trying to explain the massive destruction of Catholic schools, clinics, and churches in the Leopoldville riots—one is appalled as he drives along the street to see hundreds of thousands of dollars' damage to the very institutions serving Africans —Fernand Demany, the Belgian author of *S O S Congo* (Brussels, 1959), writes: "It was not then because they were Catholic that the missions were attacked in Leopoldville, but because they were European, and because they were too imprudently linked with the power cliques of commerce and state." He continues to warn, "It seems to us that the missions, unjustly attacked on the events of the 4, 5, 6 of January [1959], must examine their conscience. They also, as must we all."[1]

A leading African churchman, Sir Francis Ibiam, Chairman of the All-Africa Church Conference, Principal of the famed Hope Waddell (Church of Scotland) College, and himself once a medical doctor employed as a missionary, told me how he was the first African to preach in the Presbyterian Church in Salisbury, Southern Rhodesia, September 6, 1959. "I must say that I was frank and blunt in my humble message. . . . But if one cannot be outspoken and candid among Christians or those who openly confess Christianity, I am sure I do not know where else one can." In that sermon, this Nigerian leader active in the World Church warned, "Let Britain and the English-speaking peoples, who call themselves Christian, look into this matter [cultural haughtiness] with the greatest urgency and settle accounts with Africa and her people. Otherwise, unfortunate events will overtake them as sure as the day follows the night. It is well for the Universal Church to take note of these happenings and speak against them."

If our friends speak thus, what can we expect from our enemies?

Let me hasten to say that I grew up in that branch of Christianity which thought of missionaries as the purest Christians. They were the only ones who took Christ seriously and, forsaking all, went forth into the world to identify themselves with the lost and needy. They alone were the modern equivalents of the saints and martyrs, hence the real heroes of every little Protestant boy. This traditional image, applicable to Africa, has been aptly described:

We have to see in this Africa of the "day-before-yesterday" that the missionary, who was, in most cases, the first embodiment of the Church to the African, was to the African guide, philosopher and friend, and also guardian. It was the missionary who provided the African with education and healing. It was the missionary who was the uncompromising foe of the slave-trader, and when "legitimate" commerce took the place of the slave-trade the missionary sometimes pioneered it, and in general stood *in loco parentis* attempting to prevent the exploitation of the African. Again the missionary was often the interpreter to the African of the intentions and sometimes unintelligible instructions of the government.

That was the old pattern. In a few very remote areas it lingers on even today.[2]

No one can deny the heroic humanism in missions. Hardship, loneliness, disease, and death was the lot of the missionaries as they sought to bring truth, health, freedom, and dignity to individuals in every nook and corner of the world, as they educated for literacy, as they freed peoples from superstitions and bad governments, as they lifted womanhood and the socially outcast, as they spread hygiene and health and farming methods and useful crafts. These have been the by-products of the passion that impelled Christians into the world to witness for their Savior and to bring his abundant life to all men.

But the missionary gospel, as is true of all blessings, was not an unmixed blessing. The shortcomings of the missionaries are presently catching up with them: "Their divided churches—those who so love each other still love to fight one another." "Their irrelevant gospel—preparing for another world while the one under our feet is stolen from us and is wasting away." "The snobbery of a western white culture which superimposed itself upon us without either an appreciation of our culture or a willingness to bend itself to the expression of our best." These are the rumblings of the new Africa, statements actually published during 1959.

We cannot brush away these charges easily. We must listen to the African critic. To call into question some of the acts and representatives of Christianity is not necessarily to indulge in that favorite game of western secularists called "missionary-baiting."[3] It is rather to try to assess fairly the value of their work in Africa. If those who love missionaries and respect missions do not rethink matters, we may be sure that others will. Already they have assailed missions—with some truth in their barbs. Already missionaries have been forced to leave Guinea, Sudan, and Somaliland. The criticisms come from three directions: from some missionaries themselves and from some Africans within the Church, from the African elite as it becomes reflective and instated with power, and from the western secularist. At the moment in Africa all three of these elements are reappraising the Christian missionary movement. And let no one think that in the new Africa any words are minced. I was told by an African who ranks alongside the top five churchmen of the continent, who is himself a product of missions and is at the moment paid by mission money, that "many of us wish that Almighty God had left us Africans as we were and had found some other means [than westerners] to bring us the saving light of his gospel."

Yet that same African affixed his signature to the message of the first All-Africa Church Conference which read in part: "We thank God for the way that the gospel has been brought to so many countries and are filled with astonished joy that it has transformed the lives of so many men and women of Africa"! When they proceed to say that "the churches of Africa would be happy to welcome men and women of *true* missionary zeal" they obviously mean missionaries in the long tradition from Mary Slessor and David Livingstone to Dr. George Harley and Dr. Albert Schweitzer.

All the same they are insistent that "until Africa and its peoples are received by the Church and the world with open arms, and on equal terms, Christian evangelism in Africa will continue to have a rough passage." While it is good to remember that over the years the Church has been the most influential institution in provoking the changes which are now taking place in Africa— has been the herald of freedom, good will, justice, morality, equality, and security for all men—we must not forget the causes within the Church for the growing resentment against Christianity. We must become aware that this resentment, hesitant and vague in some areas but lively and outspoken in others, presents missions with perhaps its greatest world challenge. The options before the African are *live* ones, and Christianity must alert itself to the new battle of ideologies: where tribalism, racism, Islam, nationalism, Pan-Africanism, communism, and educationalism contend. This means that the Church, especially western missions, must reorient itself in terms of the present challenges of Africa.

Let us examine first some of the general criticisms made by Africans. Sir Francis Ibiam, the Nigerian, speaking before the first East Asia Christian Conference meeting in Malaya, May, 1959, declared: "But I am very sad to say that our main difficulties lie with some of our European missionaries and colleagues. To many of them, Africa must stay where she is—the baby of the world, not only in political affairs, or in economic matters, or sociologically, but even in church life and Christian emancipation." When I asked him in person about this, he replied, "Left to the African, we could move. It is the missionary who stands in our way." In the speech referred to, he went on to say:

Some missionaries do not want to build up indigenous churches at all. Some do not believe in what they call "newfangled ideas and methods." And others cannot bear to see power—administrative or monetary power—pass out of their hands and reach. To us who are African-born and very happy to belong to Africa, we cannot understand such a philosophy. One can readily understand this philosophy coming from an incorrigible and diehard imperialist or an insatiable and greedy capitalist with monopoly rights and business tentacles everywhere and all over the place doing everything in his power, wise or foolish, to make Africa stay put. But NOT an avowed Christian—one who has dedicated himself before God to a life of missionary service.[4]

In South Africa, Seth Mokotimi, African superintendent of the large Transkei Methodist district, took pains to indicate for me the common misconceptions held by some missionaries with regard to indigenous African churches. "The white European doesn't know or bother to find out about sectarians. He studies them, yes, but doesn't associate with them or welcome them into his circles. . . . South Africa is cursed by old-line denomination-alism, with its crusted divisions. . . . The African intelligentsia is leaving Christianity, *not* so much for intellectual reasons as be-cause of European-dominated churches."

In West Africa the principal of a teachers' college spent an afternoon unfolding his criticisms, even though at the moment he was attending as a lay member the week-long committee of his church: "The missionaries came to us, worked for us, toiled beside us, *but* they would not *live* among us. They build their houses on the hill. They do not mix freely. Therefore they do not know what the people think and feel. Therefore the African will not confide in him. The African seldom tells the missionary exactly what he thinks. He is too courteous."

The truth in this charge of separateness is fairly obvious. Even the casual visitor to Africa observes how many hills belong to the white man where he lives isolated, insulated in his com-pound existence. There are many justifiable reasons for this but none that assuages the African feeling of being slighted. Add to that the still common missionary reference to natives as "pagans," "heathens," and "savages," and one more easily under-stands the growing resentment. A casual, traditional reference hides a multitude of inappreciation for the African contribution to world culture.

The principal continued: "The illiterate African never makes the distinction between the man [European] in the shop, the man in the government house, and the man in the mission com-pound. They all seem to live well and make money. And in a crisis this is proven, for they all stick together, don't they?" Re-garding the last charge, there is a widely circulated account of what the famous Zulu warrior said to a missionary in the midst of the native wars. When the final showdown came between the white man and the African troops, a missionary tried to intervene in behalf of mercy and peace. In majestic disdain, Dingaan the Zulu Chief looked down upon the missionary who was piteously imploring on his knees, and said, "But even you will side with the white man in the end!"

The foregoing are typical of the charges made by the friends of Christianity, those who have been recipients and who still support the missionary. There are, however, far more scurrilous attacks made by Africans who are unalterably opposed to missionaries. In Central Africa, the African National Congress circulated accusations against the missionaries which included the old stand-by: "In the beginning we had the land and the missionary the Bible; now we have the Bible and they have the land." More sophisticated writers, like the autobiographical authors Orizu and Ojike of Nigeria, say it differently. Orizu writes: "European missionaries in Africa are more of a social and cultural liability than an asset to the Africans. . . . [They] have distorted our culture, misrepresented us, miseducated us . . . [introduced a] religious intolerance which was unknown and is undesirable in Africa."[5] Ojikes urges, "For the good of humanity, a gradual withdrawal of Western missionaries from Africa is highly desirable. . . . At present, the idea of Western Christian missionaries is comparable to that of European imperialists—to perpetuate Africa as a child who must be led by the adult hand."[6] Another African told me, "Missionaries on the field, in varying degrees, almost unconsciously share the attitudes of the controlling power. Perhaps it is fairer to say that they hope Africans will realize these aspirations 'some day,' but now 'they are children.' "

In South Africa a nicely printed pamphlet is widely circulated, called "The Role of the Missionaries in the Conquest." Written pseudonymously (some think by a product of a mission school), it is a well-documented attack against missionaries assisting the colonization of that country. A doctoral dissertation submitted in 1959 for a history degree at the University of Witwatersrand summarizes the achievements of missions from 1799-1853: "The result of a half-century was a triple failure. . . . The positive achievement of the missions in Kaffirland was to

prepare a selected number of the amaxhosa for assimilation by
the Western European culture through the introduction of Western civilizing techniques, and to prepare the way for Western
colonial expansion and the corrosion of tribal life."[7]

The signs of reaction are seen even more clearly in the decision of the non-European student body of Ft. Hare College,
which was born of missionary parents, to cease making its annual
walk-pilgrimage to the nearby monument-site of its founder.
Scorn and derision were heaped by the students upon this
effort to keep alive the missionary tradition. Instead, when this
occurred in 1959, substitutionary tribal rites took place within
two miles of the college.

Yet, all the while this criticism has been mounting from
within and without, there have been leading voices among the
missionaries themselves calling for corrections in policy. As long
ago as the Le Zoute Conference of 1926, Dr. J. H. Oldham
warned that "missionaries would, despite their physical presence
in Africa, drift outside the real life of the Continent, unless they
bore their witness among the new forces which were reshaping
the lives of the African peoples." Well known also is the famous
challenge of the missionary doctor for a half-century in West
Africa, Walter Miller:

> In a previous book of mine I made a challenge to the Missions and
> all European missionaries to leave Nigeria and hand over the direction
> and control, which they had held too long, to the Nigerian Church.
> In fear and trembling I made the challenge nine years ago. My fears
> are stronger and more insistent now, but some such test there must be.[8]

So he wrote in his controversial book, *Have We Failed in Nigeria?* (1947). Still, twenty years since his original challenge, the
majority of missionaries in Nigeria are reluctant to do so. The
"foreignness" of the missionary was deplored in the Willingen
Conference of 1952: "[The gospel] cannot be recognized as long
as it appears in a foreign guise, imitating and reproducing the
characteristics of a church in some remote and alien land. For-

eign in one sense the Church must always be; its citizenship is in heaven, and it is an agent of transformation. Despite the dangers of identification with this world, we urge that foreignness in the more earthly sense of the word is something to be outgrown with all possible speed."

The need for an alteration of Christian missionary policy in Africa does not reach the advanced stage of abandoning "missionaries" and using "fraternal workers," much less the policy of missionaries being allowed to intermarry and to nationalize themselves. No, Christianity in western dress in Africa has still to make the beginning steps, such as allowing missionaries to live away from the compounds among the Africans, to send their children to the local public schools, even to ride the local "Mammy Wagons." In theory, all the boards may say they allow these things, but in practice few do so—and then at the expense of frowns from their colleagues.

A new missionary to Ghana was so irate in the face of the traditional mold being superimposed upon him as he reported for duty in 1959 that I asked him to write his objections:

My chief disagreement is that we are forced to live *above* the very ones we have come to communicate God to. I still have to be convinced the *pedestal* is necessary: I've been told it is from Virginia to Bgotanga, but we have denied it at every juncture. I have tried to say as lovingly as I know how to every person in Ghana that the gap between missionary and masses is too wide and the imperative step in evangelization would be to narrow this gap. This places the responsibility first of all on the missionary; he must move nearer in language, housing, transportation, food, clothing, in companionship and commonness, and without love even these would be empty mockery. Our own battle began before we arrived, but intensified after we landed. Being served by "boys," having "boy" do everything for you even to lifting one's pencil! We've been in a spirit of revolt against the traditional missionary role.

All this may sound like "old stuff" to those persons keeping abreast of the more enlightened missionary policy. But we cannot remind ourselves too often that missions in Africa are still predominantly in the hands of those who follow nineteenth-century sectarianism. To be sure, there is agitation for reform within many of these bodies. Their voices are lonely and often suppressed. But they will be heard if Christianity matches the hour in Africa.

Let us look more closely at four of the most frequent criticisms of Christianity in Africa, and see if anything is being done to correct them. Foremost among them is the charge that missions lack a positive, unified approach to culture change. Dr. Emory Ross, the eminent missionary leader on African affairs, has sufficiently defined this shortcoming:

> But in the African tradition religion is not and simply cannot be dissociated from these other aspects, all aspects, of life. Therefore when these other aspects of Western life cause what the African feels are inequalities, hardships, and injustices, his experience with animism tells him that Christianity, as the religion of the people who are responsible for these things, is at bottom to blame. And when that religion, represented through the church, hesitates or refuses to denounce and work against these abuses publicly and clearly, and sometimes gives what seems to him the very lame excuse that the "spiritual" church cannot, as such, battle these other concerns that are "secular"—a distinction unknown and unacceptable to the African in his traditional society—he is profoundly shocked.[9]

How embarrassing this may be is exemplified in an occasion such as the one when Africans called upon the Secretary of the Christian Council of Leopoldville. They requested him to petition his government (in this case, British) to intervene on behalf of their freedom. Nothing he could say trying to explain the impropriety of such intervention on the part of the church or of his government satisfied them. "Didn't Britain, France, and the others sit at the table [Berlin, 1884] to divide and subdue us? Didn't the church gain by those agreements? Then, why can't you come now to aid us in our distress and to free us?"

On the positive side of the historical ledger of missions, it can be said that more and more mission policy has become aware of this spurious separation of spheres—sacred/secular—and has broadened its scope. True, oftentimes this alteration was *forced* upon them by local circumstances. For instance, they were forced to displace the medicine-man-priest with the doctor. They discovered that establishing schools for future chieftains was a shrewd but successful technique of converting from the top down. They found that they needed artisans for their own compounds and that the European overlords most readily accepted trained natives; therefore industrial education. One early missionary stated it positively: "I do not see how you can raise man's spiritual life unless you raise his bodily life to correspond." Africa being largely rural and depending upon an agrarian economy helped some missionaries to see "the healing of the land" as well as "the healing of the soul."

I visited Asaba, just west of the Niger, where Kenneth Prior, a veteran agricultural missionary, inaugurated in 1938 his now world-renowned experiment under the Church Missionary Society (Anglican). From a slow, careful beginning when he elicited local African understanding and co-operation, he eventually received support from world philanthropic organizations. His project came to receive about $500,000 for its first ten-year period, one of the two largest sums ever promised by a government to a Protestant enterprise in Africa. It developed into an agricultural experiment station on the grassroots level, using Christian staff, with a Christian atmosphere and motivation. Its benefits were open to all the members of the community irrespective of their faith. Today it has become government-managed and is going through the transitional period from mission ownership to government ownership. The hope is that such good relations have been established that missionary personnel will still be welcomed.

Although there is much to be thankful for in the changing policy with regard to a more positive, unified approach to the redemption of man-in-culture, one could wish that missionaries had had a wider sense of "vocation" in the true biblical sense. Traditional emphasis fell upon the preacher, the doctor and nurse, the teacher, as the proper vocation for the converts. These received priority, and missions promoted them in schools and overseas scholarships. But why did not the Church bless the labor organizer, the political aspirant, the journalist, the agricultural worker, and the trader? Must it repeat the same mistakes in Africa that have already blighted the secular West?

A second typical accusation against Christian missions is that many willfully or unwittingly tend to identify Christianity with the West and the Church with colonial powers. For many missionaries colonialism was the greased rail upon which to push the gospel gravy train. It may turn out to be the biggest single barrier on the obstacle course to the Christianization of Africa.

The African critic will likely not bother to check the history of a relationship which has been quite checkered, sometimes sharply opposed to government policy and taking the cause of the African to the government centers of the West. For instance, mission pioneers in South Africa were regularly accused by both the colonial government and the local colonists for being pro-African. In contrast, it was the missionaries in East Africa who had penetrated deep into the interior who urged the reluctant home government to establish imperial domination and protection over both the native and the mission station. As has been said, the pattern of relationships between missions and governments has been highly checkered, not only between regions and epochs, but also between the various denominational approaches.

Sometimes it is a subtle alignment. For instance, I called an Anglican priest's attention to the fact that in all the prayers I attended in his African churches I found them praying for the "Queen." Not once had I heard prayers for "freedom," for "African Prime Ministers," or for "the House of Chiefs." Somewhat taken aback, he produced the answer that "in some of our vernacular services we have inserted prayers for local authorities." He still did not seem to get the point.

The merits and demerits of colonialism so far as it affects missions are beyond the scope of this study. There is no need to beat a dead horse. For where it is not dead it is pulling a short haul. Far more important for the immediate future, though seen by few people as yet, is the emerging situation under the newly independent nation-states. The dilemma in the past for Protestants was whether to bite the hand that fed it: for whatever may be said against the colonial governments, they tended to favor, except in Catholic-dominated Congo, Angola, Mozambique, and in French-neutral territory, the Protestant point of view. (Another exception is where the Moslems were favored.) It was a case of a decided minority religion, imported from the outside, being given the privileges and the prestige. Now Protestant Christianity has to face the possibility of Islam swamping the new nation-states, especially where universal suffrage with bloc-voting prevails; or of the secular nation-states banning missions altogether; or of surrendering to a more political-conscious Catholic constituency. Protestants, divided as they are and overwhelmed by the quietistic withdrawal and other-worldly attitudes of the sectarians, will hardly be able to swing political opinion in their favor. Already in the Cameroons where Catholics and Protestants share about equally the minority position of Christianity, Protestants have only five or six Assembly members while Catholics have fifty or sixty. In Moslem-dominated Guinea and Sudan, missionaries are being expelled and turned away. The day of the minority religion controlling the show is over. Christianity will have to survive in a pluralistic or hostile culture if it is to survive in Africa.

That seems a strange destiny for the religion which won more converts in Africa in its last hundred years of missionary work than in all the nonwestern world. All is not lost, however. Western-introduced Christianity still holds a trump card. It laid the ground floor, educating the new leaders and spreading basic attitudes of integrity, of respect for others, and knowledge of party-democracy. It stabilized languages and cultures, and introduced a world perspective. It reached down to women and the unfortunate, often making no distinction between persons, and brought a new dignity to the little man. All this cannot be wiped out in a day.

But all this leads to a third frequent charge made by the new self-conscious African. The defender of "the African personality" is offended by the conscious and unconscious identity of Christianity with western civilization. An older Congolese Christian cornered me one night in a missionary's home and, fired with emotion, he accused missionaries of "justifying anything in order to defend European civilization. Preserving stability [of the status quo] means defense of the westerner, European missions included. Does not the missionary see that this vaunted 'stability' is guaranteed at the price of arms, altogether in favor of the outsider?"

John Taylor, the emerging spokesman for the new African in English missionary policy and a leader in the Church Missionary Society, puts it bluntly: "God is not interested in the survival of Western civilization as such."[10] Yet I heard the professor of missions in the most famous of the seminaries of Africa challenge this thesis. To him, the old trilogy—Commerce, Civilization, and Christianity—is inseparable. What is perhaps more unfortunate are the many missionaries completely blind to this unholy alliance. The gospel-jingles they sing, the Sunday school cards printed in the West (with chimneys for African children to color!), and the intimate customs they inculcate, such as the missionary who tried to persuade African women to use standard blue and pink for their newborn babies—how subtle is creeping westernization! Still we must be fair: that the national must become an ineffective imitation of the foreigner the best missionaries have never accepted as a conclusion either in theory or in practice. More and more missionaries are coming to agree with John Taylor about the deep African resentment against total westernization. He writes: "It is the gravest possible mistake for Europeans to suppose, because of the incredible technological success of modern Western civilization, that other cultures can offer no desirable alternative. Europe has learnt one way of looking at the world; Africa has another way. The white man must at least respect the African's right to be different, even if he is too slow to realize how much the world needs the African vision."[11] The missionary who returns home to display dolls collected from

world travel and invariably concludes with snide remarks about
the obvious plainness of the "primitive African doll"—measuring
it against the adornment of other cultures, especially the fanci-
ness of American dolls—misses the point, and will soon miss the
opportunity to witness to the new African personality.

At the moment there is a deliberate effort on the part of the
World Council of Churches and of certain missionary organizations to preserve the peculiar contribution that Africans can make
to religion. The Catholics have perhaps best done this, but at the
moment all over Africa there is a renewed attempt to devise "the
Africanization of Christianity." Indigenous sectarians have origi-
nated their own version of this.

An example is the Aiyetoro community on the coast of Nigeria.
It came into being in 1947 when a group of Ijale fishermen decided to take the New Testament literally, particularly in regard
to daily worship, submission to the guidance of the Holy Spirit,
and the practice of communal living. Gathering together people
of many denominations, they drew up a plan calling for severe
group discipline, then "cast themselves on the Lord." Today,
through hard work, simple living, and openhanded hospitality,
they have achieved a way of life that has been hailed in the secular press as having developed from "an extreme of austerity to a
standard of plain comfort certainly unequaled on so wide a scale
by any town in this part of Africa."

The spontaneity with which the community arose reminds one
of the Jesus Families in modern China or the Brotherhoods of
the Kingdom in Japan or Koinonia Farm in Georgia. If one were
to seek for the experiment's historical roots he could perhaps find
them in the left wing of the Reformation. But the fact is that
these simple, almost illiterate African fisherfolk had no knowledge whatever of any such historical or contemporary patterns.
It was through immediate inspiration from the Bible and from
God that they conceived and founded their "intentional community."

For the most part a self-contained economic unit, the people
of Aiyetoro hold their property in common. Profits from the sale

of surplus fish are placed in the community purse, and anyone is welcome to suggest how the funds should be spent. Through careful planning, much of the surplus has been invested in housing and machinery.

The members eat together in common dining rooms. The men and women marry, but the men live in one part of the settlement, the women in another. Polygamy, a bothersome problem in African churches, is not encouraged, but neither is it forbidden. The care and training of children conforms to traditional African practice. Each age group constitutes a social unit whose members are schooled in their privileges and responsibilities. In contributing their labor to needed community projects, the people of Aiyetoro follow the practice of tribal villages. By so doing they have constructed a seven-mile canal, built board walks and houses, woven fish nets, and installed net-drying racks. Each member is free to choose the trade he will follow—but choose he must, for idleness is not permitted.

The avowed belief is that if they wait and pray the answer to any problem will be made clear. An observer of the amazing community has written: "Many people would find it impossible to agree with them on philosophical matters. But when such methods have been applied with apparent success to the maintenance of diesel engines and an ambitious electrical plant, the premise becomes of even greater interest."

Aiyetoro seems to have solved in part the most critical problem facing Christianity in Africa: how to adapt the genius of the gospel to the African situation. These humble fishermen waited for no word from any world assembly on the church and rapid social change. They simply set to work to adapt the gospel as they understood it to the traditional homogenous tribal life. Above all, they have not allowed the adoption of Christianity to split asunder the sacred unity of the primitive community.

It may be a long time before missions cast off the Livingstone pattern—exemplified in an early society's aim, "To establish centres of Christianity and Civilization for the promotion of true religion, agriculture and lawful commerce." But a speedy adjustment must be made if external workers for Christianity expect to reach the new African.

A fourth major charge against missions is that Africans have not been allowed enough self-direction. Sir Francis Ibiam makes this his major contention, as we have noted before. Put more bluntly by an ordinary national, it reads: "Missionaries never had a policy of helping Africans reach the top of the tree." It is true that devolution, the announced policy of many boards, is moving too slowly. Too little, too late, is largely the situation. The key question is not intermarriage and naturalization on the part of mission workers, but when will western missionaries allow the African to place three members on a committee of five, when will they allow the African to handle the finances, when will they allow the African to become headmaster of the school and be willing to work themselves as subordinates? These are the urgent, first prerequisites, before we jump to the principle of complete nationalization and to the revolutionary conception of fraternal workers, coming from the younger churches as well as from the older, in a bilateral witness. Otherwise Africa may become another China.

What progress has been made in this direction has not been fast enough to allay the widespread grievance expressed by many Africans, including those who have apparently reached the top. Although Africa has as yet produced no major world theologian, they do have some outstanding churchmen: Dr. M'Timkulu, first secretary of the All-Africa Church Conference; Sir Francis Ibiam, chairman of the same; professors in the divinity schools of Ghana and Nigeria, such as Dr. Christian Baeta and Dr. Edmond Ilogu; Dr. John and Mrs. Rena Karefa-Smart of Sierre Leone (the latter perhaps the leading woman Christian of Africa); Canon Zulu and Superintendent Seth Mokotimi, leaders in their respective churches, Anglican and Methodist, in South Africa; and Africans taking leadership roles in the new ecumenical centers of Mindola in Northern Rhodesia and Limuru in Kenya. Unfortunately some of them cherish the grievance that they arrived *in spite of,* rather than with the full assistance of, the missionaries. I spent one miserable evening, feeling guilty over the behavior of my fellow missionaries, as I listened to one prominent African churchman unfold the series of discriminations against himself. He was seldom "let in" on committee decisions—"I arrived only to find that the major matters had already been decided by them in advance caucuses." He was not given equal terms of service, even when he did not seek equal treatment or equal salary. His was more than the routine tale of ups and downs of mission life.

His personalized version is fully documented by the seasoned conclusion of Dr. Emory Ross: "But one must conclude that today the Protestant staff in Africa, overwhelmingly white at the top, is critically behind its duty in this matter of giving real responsibility to African Christians in the African church."[12] He thinks this greatly explains why few good young Africans offer themselves for the ministry. "In the African church the invitation too often is to become the sub-assistant to a white foreigner forever—and in the fast-moving days of African youth even a short time that is too long can seem forever—the church will undoubtedly lose place, people, and power in these formative days of African new life."

There is too much sting in the accusation against missions made by my protagonist in the Congo: "Missionized Christians are hothouse Christians; not jungle plants. Now we are entering a new epoch when African Christianity is up against the entangling jungle plants of cheapened European Christianity and false nationalism. We must have a better variety of Christian."

There is no need to complain that "the poor savages should show more gratitude." No need to regret that "as soon as we taught them literacy, they used it to write diatribes against us." We should rejoice that they are able to stand on their own feet and talk back. The sooner they become aware of their own responsibility for Christian character, Christian evangelism in their own homeland, and Christian criticism, the happier missionaries should be that their work is coming to an end. Missions in Africa cannot build a new Africa on the memories of past accomplishments. "New occasions teach new duties."

It ill behooves missionaries who have secured and hoarded privileges all along to warn Africans of the pitfalls of the future. I was told how a white preacher was haranguing his African congregation: "You think independence will do you good and make you happy? No! You think if you live on 'high street' you will have pleasure? No! You think when your child is in the university things will improve? No!" The congregation booed him outright, much to his surprise. He left mumbling about their ingratitude. Little did he understand that when he had all these privileges—freedom, a house on high street, university education—and treasured them for himself, he was in no position to advise others while closing the door to them.

I put exactly this question to that great South African historian, whose book *The City of God and the Politics of Crisis* is a classic for understanding religion in Africa: "Who can assist the African Christian in these perilous days ahead, when he distrusts everyone, even those who have helped him?" "Only that Christian is capable of guiding the African who has in and before his own white associates unrelentingly opposed their reluctance, their snobbery, and their oppression," was the reply of Edgar Brookes.

The voice of the true missionary will yet be heard in the New Africa. The Christian missionaries left a legacy of friendships, education, and acceptable western institutions and ideas. The Christian Church is rooted in numerous African communities. But in no case can the Christian forces rest on their laurels or use the same methods. Africa is critical.

4
nationalism

● ● ● ● ● ● ● ● ● ●

Nationalism is the rash that has broken out on the body of Africa. Within this decade more nation-states will have come into existence than at any time in the continent's history, perhaps in the world's history. The unrestrained nationalism that brings these countries into being will be severely tested, as to the type and stability of self-government. The supreme test, though, is whether African nationalism can keep open the frontiers that the outside forces of colonialism and Christianity cut through the jungle of closed, suspicious tribal communities.

The success or failure of African nationalism depends upon the kind of nationalism that wins. Will it be a nationalism restrained and internally corrected by a transcendent Christian value system? Or a nationalism that subordinates itself to Pan-Africanism so that the benefits of a united nations for Africa will prevail? Or a selfish black nationalism that destroys itself hating both the malefactors and benefactors of the colonial past and splitting itself upon tribal jealousies? In any case, nationalism seems to be that inevitable childhood disease as Africa takes its place in the adult world of power states.

Some observers fear that it is mostly black nationalism, fed primarily by anti-white hate. Its fervor and what unity it has are derived from the pent-up feelings of the black man against his exploiters, sometimes specified as "the military, the mercenary, and the missionary." The fact is that its very leaders are not above appealing to this motif. Awolowo, one-time prime minister of Western Nigeria, put it bluntly: "For be it remembered that the fire of nationalism cannot burn without fuel—and grievances (real and imaginary) are its readiest fuel."[1] One of the last sentences of Nkrumah's autobiography reads: "Our task is not done . . . until the last vestiges of colonialism have been swept from Africa."[2] Dr. Hastings Banda seized the leadership of Nyasaland's independence movement and won his place in prison with these words: "Go to your prisons in your millions, singing Hallelujah! The European has had his opportunity to lead Africans, and has lost it. To hell with white rule." The Accra All-Africa People's Conference set the note: "Civilized or not, ignorant or illiterate, rich or poor, we deserve a government of our own choice." Tom Mboya claims: "The Europeans want me to agree that Kenya is different from Ghana. I won't agree. They are fundamentally the same despite the existence of a handful of European settlers. Kenya is an *African* country."

Expressions such as these no doubt strike a responsive chord in all Americans who have thrilled to the memories of our own fight against foreign feet on our soil, but that there are pitfalls along a narrow nationalist path we all must admit. Not all the younger nationalists are as generous as the Union of South Africa's Chief Luthuli, who told me in an interview granted under the adverse circumstances of his third arrest in ten years for political agitation that "I am willing for any person to remain who calls himself an African." The rallying cry, "Africa for Africans," can be so restricted that it means what one young leader yelled: "I am so African that I cannot imagine anybody not black living in Africa."

Pan-Africanism is the positive force that seeks to convert the negative expression of nationalism. The two most nationalistic leaders of Africa have embraced it, indeed are vying with each other to command it. Nkrumah recounts how in the hour of his Ghana triumph he "drove home, physically and mentally tired but indescribably happy and content . . . From now on it must be Pan-African nationalism, and the ideology of African political consciousness and African political emancipation must spread throughout the whole continent, into every nook and corner of it. I have never regarded the struggle for the independence of the

Gold Coast as an isolated incident but always as a part of a general world historical pattern."[3]

Nasser in an early paper setting forth his ideals for Egypt wrote similarly: "We cannot under any circumstance remain aloof from the terrible and sanguinary struggle going on in Africa today between five million whites and 200 million Africans. . . . I will continue to dream of the day when I will find in Cairo a great African Institute dedicated . . . to an enlightened African consciousness and to sharing with others from all over the world in the work of advancing the peoples of the continent."[4] His dream is expressed at the moment in the powerful radio station beaming its propaganda in twenty-five languages southward.

Presidents Tubman of Liberia and Toure of Guinea and the prime ministers of the three regions of Nigeria have all declared themselves for Pan-Africanism. Even the historic "Lion" of Ethiopia, traditionally a go-it-aloner, stole the march on the Accra Conference (1958) with his offer of fifty scholarships to his new university for students from any African country.

Still Pan-Africanism is more a word than a movement, although it is assuming some of the features of the latter. It has its saint. George Padmore who gave himself unstintingly to the dream has his ashes enshrined in the buttresses of Christiansborg Castle with this arousing epitaph, "Had I more than one life to live I would spend it for Africa." During his short years he helped organize five congresses to promote the spirit and wrote books to expand the idea. He held that Pan-Africanism "offers an ideological alternative to Communism on the one side and Tribalism on the other. It rejects both white racialism and black chauvinism."[5]

It has its music. Almost everywhere on the continent in Africa South one can hear the strains of the militant song "Let Africa Return" and the hymn that so often accompanies it, "God Bless Africa." I first heard it (the latter) sung at a theological school in Kenya, again at candidate Garfield Todd's interracial political rally in Salisbury, then at a backward country school in South Africa where I was paying a popcall. It is almost universal, and wherever it is sung it enlists every voice. "Nkosi Sikeleli Afrika" is the melodious first line of the Zulu recording I possess.

It has its conferences. The first was the Accra All-Africa Political Conference. Then the All-Africa Economic Conference and the 1959 All-Africa Peoples' Conference. It is said that no meeting would be a success in Africa today without being heralded as "All-Africa." In late 1958 the All-Africa Church Conference came into being. It was my privilege to be living in the home of Dr. M'Timkulu, on the faculty of Ft. Hare College, South Africa, the very day the world press released the news of his appointment as the first secretary of that organization. In a tape-recorded interview I captured some of the thrill that was his at that moment.

Pan-Africanism is definitely a continental mood. It is a bandwagon on which all the nationalists bent on their separate ways must swing aboard. It is a force to be reckoned with. It may have its limitations, it may have its internal splits, it may be more a mood than a movement, but it is the only ideology at the moment uniquely African and capable of mustering the heretofore tribally isolated African to an overarching loyalty. One of its best utterances is that of a young South African leader: "Our nationalism must transcend the barriers of nationality and geography and discover in the peoples of Africa brothers in a common struggle to assert the dignity of Africans."

Everybody admits the road to a United States of Africa is rough, perhaps impossible. Already it has hit some rocky places. Guinea and Ghana are nowhere near working agreements. Nigeria is not likely to listen to little Ghana, because in traditions, size, and diversity it has its own ideas. Multifragmentalization and strident local nationalism may in the long run outpace unionism. Even so, the dream of a working unity for Africa, born from an internal affinity rather than superimposed by world powers, is welcomed by the democratic world. And could it not be that Christianity with its ripened doctrine of supranationalism provides Africans with a motivation other than anti-white, anti-colonial feelings? Africa of the future will need a positive motivation and a creative policy more than it needs a negative protest, and Christianity could well fill the gap.

Nationalism, Pan-Africanism, freedom, and politics are all in the air of Africa. One cannot help being invigorated by the excitement and expectation, though sometimes the atmosphere is polluted by overzealous and amateurish devotees. I asked to see the "Freedom tree" in Uganda, at the market plaza in Kampala where the boycott against non-African goods was initiated. I stood with the students at the University of Cape Town in "freedom corner," on the main quadrangle overlooking the vast wastes of Cape flats where Indians, Colored, and Africans languish. Upon arriving in Accra I was taken posthaste to Freedom Arch on which are emblazoned the words "Freedom and Justice," the motto of Ghana, the nation that put the torch to Africa's freedom fire. And to be in Nigeria where I lectured in those reckless days before the general elections of 1959 was to share the penultimate of modern nationalism. People not only named their lorries "Freedom" but planned their babies to be born in 1960! But the story that tops the list comes from Kenya. "Uhuru" is the Swahili word for freedom and is the salutation everywhere, just as the upturned thumb is the signal of the South African Nationalist Congress. The story goes that at a mission school which the chief's son attended, the little fellow had broken a serious rule and had to be punished corporally. As he was bending to receive the blows, instead of crying he yelled at the impact of each stroke, "Uhuru! Uhuru!"

Politics dominates this new world of Africa. Could it be otherwise where the majority of the fifty-odd territories secure their freedom within this decade? Then, too, Africans, in spite of the long depreciation of their merits by the occupying powers, are natural politicians. They enjoy *palaver*. Theirs has long been a government by discussion. It is for this reason and others that the new African cannot understand the reluctance of Christians and of the churches to get involved. Many Africans suspect that the mission churches are against political autonomy, as one of them put it, "for fear of being driven out with the imperialist agents."

They cannot understand why some Christians share the fright
that possesses the majority of the whites in Africa in the face of
rising nationalism. As the Christian writer from Southern Rhodesia, Ndabaningi Sithole, puts it at the very outset of his book,
African Nationalism, "The average white man in Africa is scared
almost out of his senses by the rapidly emerging African nationalism. An African nationalist is regarded not only as potential but
as real danger to the present status of the white man in Africa."[6]

In this political whirlpool Christians are being compelled to
become involved, sometimes ignorantly, sometimes by default.
In the analysis that follows we shall try to be as thorough as possible in uncovering the history of Christianity's delinquency in
African politics, and of Christianity's contribution to African
nationalism, and in suggesting what Christians may do in the
future.

That Christians have been delinquent in providing guidance
for African nationalism is at last admitted. This admission issues
from Christians themselves, not merely from the enemies of Christianity. Sithole, the young Rhodesian Congregationalist preacher
whose recent book is cited above, writes: "Let it be noted right
from the outset that when the missionaries went to Africa, they
had not the slightest idea of helping African nationalism as such.
Their primary goal was to propogate the Gospel of Christ to their
fellow human beings. The Church has been only a blind instru-
ment in the whole process of African nationalism. On the whole,
missionaries in Asia and Africa have been accused, and not without cause, of standing in the way of emerging nationalism. In the
main, they have been staunch supporters of colonial rule so that
colonial powers cannot blame the rise of African nationalism on
the missionaries as a class."[7]

From the Secretary of the Christian Council of Kenya, I received this letter: "I am afraid that political leaders everywhere
have found the Churches reactionary. The more I think
about this the more I feel it is not just the theological position.
It is due mainly to the clash of generations, the missions and
Churches really representing the old generation, whereas political
leaders are, with few exceptions, relatively young. I have often

been puzzled by the fact that the Church, which was in the vanguard of progress, enlightened thinking, etc., in the early periods of African development, and as such did win the confidence of all progressive elements within the old society, has failed in a large measure to render the same service to the second generation."

At the same time a West African writes: "My observation of the African scene leads me to conclude that the Christian Church is an extremely cautious institution as far as political issues are concerned. Pronouncements on political and socio-economic affairs at international and national conferences by church bodies tend to be so general and vague that they could not be of much help to the interested Christian politician, and if they are clear and direct they come too late to do much good. To be fair to the missionary church of Africa, I should add that this cautiousness is typical of Christian churches everywhere today."

Thus from South, East, and West Africa comes the consensus that the Church has failed in this matter. We may list at least four reasons. First, Christianity entered under colonial sanction. The missionaries lived and moved and had their being within the graces of the established colonial government. They knew where their bread was buttered as they received the vast handouts for the running of their schools and hospitals. They knew how to keep quiet, even in the face of obvious injustice on occasion. This is understandable and perhaps forgivable. But that they counted on the eternality of this political arrangement is where they are subject to criticism. Many were quite willing to enjoy the red carpet laid out to them at the governmental functions, but quite unwilling to place a guiding hand of advice upon the young African aspiring to politics. I was told by more than one African that if he showed an inclination for politics, he was blackballed so far as the Church was concerned. Even some of the missionaries confirmed this by revealing that once a leading African became known for his political maneuvers he was no longer considered for mission scholarships, for church favors, for church office. He was "too hot."

This leads to the second reason for the Church's failure. All too often the missionaries on the field represent a politically irresponsible constituency back home. In their own political background they have been content, due to a distorted notion of the separation of church and state principle, to be the "goody-good" people while others run the government. They failed to see that a good man can hardly be good who forfeits his political responsibility. Gathering up their own pharisaical skirts they left politics in the hands of those whom they knew to be scoundrels. Such a negative view of politics carried over to the mission field in an even exaggerated form. Many churchmen did not want to grant to the African politician the same privilege of political levity that is granted everywhere in England and America to politicians who all the while remain members in good standing in the local churches. Must the African politician be simon-pure before he can be accepted within the Church?

I recall the looks of utter dismay that greeted my wife and myself as we emerged from Tom Mboya's Volkswagen in front of the mission house where we were staying in Nairobi. We had had breakfast with him and several prominent Africans where we talked about these very things. The missionaries were so aghast that it took them several minutes to catch their breath enough to ask if that really was Mboya. "Why, yes," we said, "don't you know him?" "No," was their haughty reply, "and pray tell us what you were doing with him"—in a manner as if we had desecrated their sacrosanct quarters. "We were making friends with him. Don't you think it is about time that Christians began chumming with the prospective leaders of Africa? We're hardly in a position to criticize till we know them and have tried to assist them."

Similarly, I recall riding with two world-traveled mission leaders in Leopoldville. As they passed the Consul-General's residence they looked at one another and asked almost simultaneously whether they should call upon His Honor. One who had been for many years in India replied, "Yes, quite so; in the old days I never dared pass up such an opportunity." This, mind you, in 1960, just before the outbreak of the Congo crisis. It is doubtful whether either of them knew a single local politician, or had even bothered to call upon them, much less influence them. These are the kind of Christians walking blindfolded into the new Africa. It could be that the Church is betting on the wrong horse.

On the other hand, their self-defense is persuasive. "You can't expect the ordinary missionary always to be going out of his way to meet every Tom, Dick, and Harry who pretends to politics. That is not our business. Our business is to win souls and to pastor the Church." This argument holds true, up to a point. The missionary, it is true, ought no more support the African in his unlimited desires for freedom in order to win concessions from him in the day of his power than he should curry favor from the present colonialism. It is the duty of Christians to be as impartial as possible, and that is a razor's edge in these trying days. But can they pretend to impartiality if at the same time they fit hand-in-glove within the existing powers and make little effort to understand and sympathize with the needs and demands of the subject people? There comes a time when Christians are obliged to make decisions in the political sphere, decisions which, besides affecting the future of their own mission, help determine the extension of justice and righteousness in the world itself. This is surely what was meant by the Belgian critic of his 1959 Congolese government when he wrote, "Those in the faith cannot serve two masters. They must choose between God and Mammon. That is to say, between the Congolese who seek liberty and the rapacious reactionaries who refuse them."[8]

A third reason for Christians not participating in African politics inheres in the practices that prevail in some sections known as "dashing" and "swearing on juju." "Dashing"—known in the West as bribery—is reportedly widespread and if so is certainly corrupting to public morals. More serious, however, is the securing of votes by getting the common people in the villages to "swear on juju" to vote for a certain candidate. In a society where swearing is taken seriously, and where "swearing on juju" is inviolable for the still superstitious masses, this can be disastrous for democracy. I was told by the English-educated headmaster of an East Nigerian secondary school that "every politician is forced to use juju to secure votes. Even if he won't do it, has scruples against it, his agents will do it in spite of his wishes. Money, bribery, is not our big problem. Ours is a lack of understanding about basic democratic individuality—one man, one vote." Christians consequently think they have an additional reason to stay out of politics: it is idolatrous.

A fourth reason emanates from the African himself. It is essential to remember that not all the opposition to Christians participating in African politics comes from the side of conservatism and passivity within the Church. African nationalists, like their counterparts elsewhere on this globe, are no more ready to embrace restraining advice and opposing power from ecclesiastical sources. All too often they are more than anxious to have the Church take their side in any movement for freedom, but once their goal is achieved they seem as definite as power-politicians anywhere that the Church should then keep "hands off." "No Church interference," is the rule of unrestrained nationalism and it applies in Africa, too. I put exactly this question to Kasavubu, the leader of the formidable Abaka Party in Leopoldville who was destined to become first president of his country: "Do you want the backing of the Church for your independence fight; and if so, what will be your attitude toward the Church in the day of your success?" He shrewdly foresaw the direction of that question and parried, "I want the Church to stay out of our way, that's all, both before and after independence. And I can assure the Church that I will not bother it." (He undoubtedly had in mind the Roman Catholic Church in which he once trained toward the priesthood and which dominates the Congo.) Nkrumah takes a similar position. In answer to a press question he replied to an interviewer in November, 1959: "The Church in Ghana should keep away from local politics but actively preach the gospel."

African politicians cannot have it both ways. Alan Paton, who surely wants freedom for the African as much as anyone, has well said, "The Church is called not only to liberate from outside control and exploitation but from excesses of nationalism from within." It is to the credit of the indigenous churches in the newest nations of Africa that they are rising to the challenge from within. The Anglican Bishop of Accra in October, 1959, made a major public pronouncement of caution before the national elections. Similarly, Bishop Howells of Lagos called together the leaders of all political parties for an hour of prayer on the eve of their city's federal elections. A good rule is that the Church in Africa must on no account espouse the cause of nationalism in order to curry favor and win the support of the masses and in the process renounce its judgmental and redemptive role.

Previous to now there has been too much silence on the part of mission churches; understandable, yes, but not entirely justifiable. Too often missionaries and even African church members remained aloof from freedom movements. Their loyalty to Christian principles, and to the Church in which all are one in Christ was mixed with undue devotion to the status quo and to "things overseas." This tended to make them suspect to the ardent nationalist. It became the belief of many that the Church is opposed to self-government. A writer from Central Africa summarized this reaction: "An attitude of silence from the Church leads to the conclusion by the African that the Church from overseas will always react in favor of its own national aspirations, and consequently an urge is given to the separatist tendency in the African mind, and the desire grows to see the Church reflecting the aspirations of the indigenous inhabitants." A local missionary writes: "The Church here tends to be very conservative and there is a feeling among the new generation that it is a museum piece belonging to the age of colonialism—a feeling which is not altogether without justification."[9] In the light of these random reports it is not surprising that a regional church conference concluded: "In the realm of modern politics and social life the influence of the Church has yet to be felt to a marked degree." The ablest authority on missions all over Africa is perhaps Max Warren of the Church Missionary Society, headquarters in London. He sustains the above conclusions:

The Church has laid very little store by its function of infiltrating the life of the State with men and women with the revolutionary fire of the Spirit in their lives. It has done even less to prepare Africans for an understanding of politics and the Christian's responsibility in and for politics. At a time when Africans are becoming more and more politically conscious, this represents a major failure on the part of the Church to exercise one of its functions in relation to the State. . . .

The young African is going with knightly courage and hope, but going, alas, without the inspiration of a vigil before God's altar, and the guidance and blessing of God's priest.[10]

Such is the record of the delinquency of Christianity with regard to rising African nationalism. Now that Africans are drunk with nationalism it is no more than natural that in her tipsy state some of them should accuse Christianity of neglect in fortifying her for her day of freedom. On the other hand, there are just as many observers, in fact some of the very critics cited above, who claim that Christianity planted the seed of independence. Where the western churchmen represented free citizens in their own persons, where their mission schools educated in the concepts of freedom, where the Bible was allowed free interpretation, it was inevitable that the leaven of freedom should ferment. A young Nigerian warned his British audience years ago: "Education means the coming sooner or later of national consciousness. The missionaries are largely responsible for the shake-up of the British Empire." Nkrumah, since his ascendancy, has on several occasions taken the trouble to pay tribute to the indirect benefit of missions.

First among these indirect benefits of Christianity was the Bible itself, which many claim is revolutionary enough. Men who share as widely divergent social views as Sir Philip Mitchell and Chester Bowles agree that this is the case. The former, who was the typical empire Britisher in his colonial office over Kenya for many years, wrote recently: "The Bible. . . . I believe to have been the decisive force in the whole business . . . the prime mover [in the liberation of Africa]."[11] Bowles, in a book summarizing his own impressions, called *Africa's Challenge to America*, declared:

"Thus the Christian missionaries and their Book have been in this very practical sense Africa's true revolutionaries."[12]

African leadership itself joins in this tribute to the influence of the Bible. Sithole raises and answers the question as follows: "What is the actual relevance of the Bible to African nationalism? . . . The Bible is redeeming the African individual from the power of superstition, individuality-crushing tradition, witchcraft, and other forces that do not make for progress. The same Bible is helping the African individual to reassert himself above colonial powers! It is inconceivable to a logical mind that the Bible could deliver the African from traditional domination without at the same time redeeming him from colonial domination."[13]

Another testimony to the effect of the Bible shows up in the uneasy truce that existed between the missionaries and the colonial powers on this very point. It is well known how the Portugese have shown consistency in restricting the entry of Protestant missions on the ground that they are the advance guard of African nationalism. Their opinion, quoted from an 'Angola journal, goes as follows: "To tell a person he is able to interpret the Bible freely is to insinuate in him an undue autonomy and turn him into a rebel. . . . A Protestant native is already disposed toward —not to say an active agent in—the revolt against civilising peoples."[14] Even missionaries themselves have been at odds over how far they should trust the African with the radical doctrines of the Bible. In the twenties a High Anglican, A. G. B. Glossop, protested against the Scottish Mission, on the occasion of the Chilembwe revolt in Central Africa, because they trusted the Africans with the Bible. The African way of life, he said, was "communistic and not individualistic"; thus to make the Bible "the sole guide of truth and doctrine was to give to the African a freedom of opinion which could not but lead ultimately to sedition."[15]

A second manifestation of the indirect contribution of Christianity to the building up of Africa has been the education of her leaders. We have noted how virtually all of the politicians were educated in mission schools. Yet at the same time this was no guarantee that they remain Christian in their lives and policies. Nonetheless, it can be expected that the friendships established, the loyalties formed, and the characters molded will have lasting effect. What is more important is that most of the articulate leaders of the new Africa, those who are writing books for their countrymen and the world, write from a Christian perspective. Here one thinks of Julius Nyerere, the nationalist leader of Tanganyika who addressed the World Council of Churches in 1959 and had the lead article in the *New York Times Magazine* in January, 1960. Or, of Dr. and Mrs. John Karefa-Smart, both high in the government of Sierre Leone and active in medicine, education, student Christian work, and ecumenical affairs, whose jointly authored book, *The Halting Kingdom,* 1959, is among the best treatments of the whole problem through African eyes. The same can be said of Sithole's *African Nationalism,* 1960, referred to so often above. Or, of the Nigerian, N. U. Akpam, who dedicated his *Epitaph to Indirect Rule* to a Presbyterian missionary who started him on his way. All these Africans are *young,* around forty; all of them are speaking for responsible statesmanship and are endeavoring to keep their fellows on the road to democratic statehood. Of course, we need not mention the architects of Black Africa's freedom; Ghana's Nkrumah, Nigeria's Azikewe, and South Africa's Chief Luthuli, two of whom were exposed to American theological education.

In this context it does not seem strange that Dr. Azikewe ended his major bid for the premiership of the new Nigeria in 1960 with this song (I will let his speech introduce it): "When I attended the Tinubu Methodist Sunday School in Lagos, I was taught to sing a song entitled 'The Golden Age,' which was composed by Walter Hawkins, and its words are so pregnant with wisdom that they have left an indelible impression on my mind since I left the Sunday School forty years ago."

> It is stage by stage to the golden age,
> Far off we seem to view it;
> But the good we crave will come to the brave
> Who see God's will and do it.

"Zik" went on to say: "All that we fought for in the drama that is coming to its climax is to enable our children to share and to enjoy a more abundant life than we did; otherwise, the struggle would be worthless." Social gospel fancifulness, yes, but history suggests that Wesleyan singing may have saved England from a French Revolution.

Thomas Hodgkin, whose book *Nationalism in Colonial Africa* is the most thorough study of the over-all setting, maintains that the ideology underlying African nationalism is borrowed largely from Christianity. Foremost is the idea of "human brotherhood and the specifically Protestant conception of an 'Elect'; the traditional democratic belief in 'right to choose our own governors, to cashier them for misconduct and to frame a government for ourselves.' "[16]

Third, bearing directly on the rise of African nationalism is the share missionaries and their home bases have contributed to "Ethiopianism," the label first applied to the African's embryonic struggle for freedom as it grew within the bosom of the Church. ("Ethiopia" because of the Scripture reference, "Ethiopia shall soon stretch out her hands unto God," Psalm 68:31, and because of rising African consciousness of this ancient monarchy possessing a national church with a tradition older than many European ones.) The beginnings of the movement lie in obscurity. In fact, the spasmodic episodes expressive of the mood actually have not had enough continuity and continent-wide uniformity to justify calling it a movement. But the mood is there, seething and threatening, and cannot be denied.

As long ago as 1829 Robert A. Young published in New York *An Ethiopian Manifesto,* "Issued in defense of the Black Man's Rights, in the Scale of Universal Freedom." Apparently it did not take hold in Africa until the latter part of the nineteenth century when the splinter movement away from the established mission churches began. A South African historian records: "It is an interesting fact that the first Bantu mass movement on truly national lines was a religious one. What came to be called Ethiopianism was an attempt on the part of Christian Africans to set up their own churches independent of white ones. . . . Though outwardly

religious, they were to a large extent political in their appeal.
They began as a revolt of the black members within the missionary churches."[17]

What is important is that this separatist movement soon established loose connections with the Negro denominations of America. For instance, the African Methodist Episcopal Church,
formed in 1816 but not gaining much headway until the end of
the century, had sponsored at least one hundred and fifty Africans from the Union in the States by 1906. Bishop Henry M.
Turner's whirlwind tour of South Africa left bitter seeds. His
1896 broadsides in favor of Africa for Africans read in part: "The
time has now come to replace them [whites], with their anti-
quated methods and superannuated principles. Our new doctrine
is more suited to the Africa awakening, and only the sons of New
Africa may be trusted to propagate it, not any aliens. Africa is
is a new land, a new world; she needs new men, and we are the
men she needs. Arise, Africa! for Ethiopia is holding out her
hands, not as a suppliant, as the white men call her, but to incite
us to throw out our arms like boxers, seize the enemy, chuck him
out and conquer the first place among peoples."[18]

Yet it remained for a white missionary to first standardize the
slogan "Africa for Africans" by the composition of a book by
that title just at the close of the nineteenth century. Writing
while on furlough in this country, Joseph Booth had already
stirred up considerable trouble in his work as an independent
missionary in central Africa. The African Christian Union he
sought to organize contained twenty-one points in its constitution, all carrying the high-sounding idealism of the radical Christian socialism gaining momentum in this country and in England.
One point read: "To unite together Christians of the African
race and of various denominations in the name of Jesus Christ to
solemnly work toward and pray for the day when the African
people shall become an African Christian nation." It began with
the Isaiah passage, "And a small one [will become] a strong
nation: I the LORD will hasten it" (60:22).

The year 1896, fortuitously it seems, became the high mark of the movement. That year witnessed the Ethiopian repulse of the Italian military overtures which aimed to swallow that ancient kingdom in the same manner as the other European partition of Africa. Later Mussolini's campaign in the thirties evoked continent-wide sympathies and a temporary revival of Ethiopianism.

Subsequently, a series of apparently disconnected episodes in Africa's history stirred the seething pot of nationalism. Charles Domingo, a Nyasaland Separatist, released a denunciatory pamphlet in 1910, reading in part: "The three combined bodies, Missionaries, Government and Companyies, or gainers of money, do form the same rule to look upon the native with mockery eyes. It sometimes startles us to see that the three combined bodies are from Europe, and along with them there is a title 'Christendom.' . . . If we had power enough to communicate ourselves to Europe we would advise them not to call themselves 'Christendom' but 'Europedom.' Therefore the life of the three combined bodies is altogether too cheaty, too thefty, too mockery."[19]

John Chilembwe, the first Nyasaland native to be educated in America, who helped Booth set up the ill-fated Providence Industrial Mission in 1901, led an uprising in 1915 to expel the Europeans. In the Congo, the Kimbangu fracas of 1921 resulted in the imprisonment of the revolutionary prophet who, according to one historian, had "excited his followers against authority . . . had even set himself up to be the Saviour of the Black Race and had called the white men his 'abominable enemy.' "[20] Such cases were infrequent but fairly widespread over the continent. For instance, about the same time, the United Native Church, an offshoot of the English Baptist, in the French Cameroons had "the whole town of Douala seething with religious 'revolt' in which natives paraded up and down the streets singing anti-European hymns." In Nigeria earlier, the United Native African Church had seceded partly in protest against the British Church Missionary Society, whose first African Bishop, Crowther, was supposed to be too friendly to Europeans. Their constitution of 1891 said, "Resolved, that a purely Native African Church be founded for the evangelization and amelioration of our race, to be governed by Africans."

By 1960, however, the older denominations and sects were so thoroughly entrenched in West Africa that the politically conceived Nigerian National Church was virtually stillborn. In South Africa it is a different story. B. G. M. Sundkler, the Swedish authority who has followed that movement there in his book *Bantu Prophets,* reports that Ethiopianism continues to be multiplying and as pressing an issue as it was in 1914 when the leading Anglicans were urging the necessity of appointing native bishops "to stem the tide." (Unfortunately their pleas were still unheeded on the occasion of the author's visit forty-five years later.) As may be expected, there are mixed motives that pervade the movement: personal ambitions, sectarian disagreements, race hatred, petty loyalties, and so forth. But the major element has been the political desire for self-direction fed by religious aspirations. Historically, separatism as a religious movement has sometimes been associated with political radicalism, sometimes with quietism. That in Africa it has lent itself to the former is due largely to the fact that here religion has been the only field within which emancipation was possible. That the old-line mission churches did not enter into and promote this mood for African autonomy has simply led to sectarianism being more rampant in Africa than anywhere else in the world. Africans have taken the Protestant principle to its extreme, and have not been reluctant to harness their political desires to it.

A more direct contribution of Christianity to African nationalism has been the intervention of missionaries and the churches in colonial affairs. All along there have been a few agitators who slipped through the fingers of colonial administrators to make the facts known to the world, to plead for justice to the African, or to generate liberation movements. Space does not allow a complete listing of these heroic voices, say from the time of Dr. John Philip in the early mission work of South Africa to the occasion of the arrest of Guy Clutton-Brock of St. Faith's Mission, the only European detained in the Rhodesian emergency of 1959.

The Church in South Africa is known the world over for its protests in the form of Father Trevor Huddleston (*Naught for Your Comfort*), the Rev. Mr. Michael Scott (*A Time to Speak*), Bishop Ambrose Reeves (*Shooting at Sharpville*), and Archbishop Joost de Blank. What is less known is that leading churchmen in the Catholic, the Methodist, the Congregationalist, the Presbyterian, and even the principal Dutch Reformed denominations have likewise made their feelings known.

The most outstanding case, in modern times, of a mission board protesting the policy of a government is that of the Church of Scotland going on record in 1959 against the mishandling of the Central Africa Federation on the part of the British. Naturally, there were voices which questioned the Church's dabbling in politics. Its mission magazine, *Other Lands* (Nov. 1959), commented in advance: " 'Keep out of this political dispute' is the advice of many people, especially those who uphold the Federation. But, of course, they mean keep out so that our policy may prevail. They don't mean have nothing to do with Federation policy either in support or opposition, they mean keep out of opposition. The dilemma of the Church of Nyasaland is this: If its ministers and members keep out of politics as a Church, this will be assumed to be indifference to the issues of politics and particularly to the basic issue—the threat to freedom as most Africans see it. It will be implied that their silence is their consent. . . . There is no contracting out of these political problems."

It is to the credit of the newly organized Christian councils that are coming into being in certain areas that they are speaking up on political issues in Africa. As early as 1949, seven European members and eight African members of the Christian Council of the Gold Coast published a joint personal statement on "Christianity and Politics" which set forth eight principles. The first was: "We recognize that the Gold Coast, like any other country, has a natural right to self-government." Momentarily, the Christian Council of Kenya has worked at length on and has submitted to the Constitutional Committee preparing for self-government its detailed suggestions. The All-Africa Church Conference, both in its plenary sessions and in its continuing committee, has applied itself vigorously to Africa's political problems. Similarly, the World Council of Churches' center at Kitwe maintains a group of experts attuned to what is happening in the continent's political pulse, especially as it relates to Christianity.

Besides Sithole, leading African churchmen are awake to Christianity's responsibility in politics. Sir Francis Ibiam pleads with his countrymen on every occasion "to act like grown men and world citizens." John V. Taylor, long a missionary expert on Africa, has written one of the most relevant books on this subject, *Christianity and Politics in Africa*. The All-Africa Church Conference in its first meeting declared: "The Church dare not assume a passive, indifferent or neutral attitude toward the crucial political and social issues of the times. It must uphold righteousness, champion the oppressed, and declare the sov ereignty of God over all creation including the institutions of man."

In many ways the Roman Catholic Church has been on its toes more than have Protestants. It has not been reluctant to make political pronouncements, to sponsor candidates, and to infiltrate or organize parties. Typical of its behavior is the section of the pastoral letter issued by the Bishops of Tanganyika in 1953, called "The People of Tanganyika and their Political Aspirations": "Nobody looks back with greater joy on the advance of Tanganyika than the Church, which has spared no pains to try to bring to Africa what is best in Christian civilization. . . . For the goal desired by all is a self-governing Tanganyika and the preparatory work in view of this is proceeding at a gradual but ever-quickening pace."

Such are the indirect and direct contributions of Christianity to African nationalism. We could also mention the fact of nonviolence which has marked all the movements and parties working for African freedom. The extraordinary aspects of this fact should not be overlooked, and surely much of this issued from

Christian preparations as well as from the knowledge of Gandhi's success in India and the resources latent in the mentality of many African tribes. Nkrumah's commitment to "positive action" or nonviolence is well known, and the latest move in the Pan-African gatherings was to appoint a body of experts to study and to guide its application to the African scene. When I interviewed Chief Luthuli, President of the South African Nationalist Congress, he had been reading that very morning Martin Luther King's *Stride Toward Freedom*. "This book," he said, "with its method of passive resistance, could save our party in South Africa. If only I had enough copies to put into the hands of all my party leaders."

Also there is the contribution that Christianity has made, in an unwitting way, to the political strategy of Africans. Strangely enough, many parties have borrowed the methods of American popular revivalism for their campaigns. Using prayers and hymns, and recasting gospel songs and motifs to fit the African situation, they have on occasion exploited revivalism to the fullest.

Now we come to the key question: What does Christianity promise for the future of African nationalism? In this fast-moving, electrically charged climate, not even the best authority would dare prophesy. I think it can be safely said, though, that as unrestrained nationalism gains momentum in the immediate years ahead, Christianity which is true to its historic and transcendent allegiance is going to be severly tested. Decidedly, it will no longer have the favored position of a minority religion in an alien land, guaranteed its status by the might of the occupying powers. It will be on its own competing against the world's most engaging ideologies.

However, as we have pointed out, there are signs that responsible indigenous leaders will provide the forum to air Africa's political problems under a more objective and transcendent light, under the sunlight that we believe the Christian gospel provides. Presently it can be said, I believe, that Christianity is becoming more realistic in the African situation and that in its recent top-level pronouncements it is as relevant to the African situation as it is anywhere in the world. It arrived Johnny-come-late with its political concern, but compared to the Church's negligence and squeamishness in politics in other parts of the world, African Christians are to be commended.

Alan Paton, who is as much an African as any white man, challenged the Church at its first All-Africa Conference in 1958: "But here is the whole world of Africa changing before our eyes; Africa is on the march, and in so far as the march has spiritual significance, the Church must be in the van. For God's sake let no one dismiss this march by calling it politics." May his words be the death knell of the old tradition of Christianity in Africa and the rising bell for its new day's work.

racism

5

• • • • • • • • • •

There is a poisonous plant in the bush country of Africa that reaches across the jungle path to infect all who come into contact with it. Once it touches the skin, its inflammation sets up an unbearable pain. Similarly, racism affects the various ideologies of Africa; none of them enters the territory without suffering its distortions. It is not so much a single ideology, as a mental disease which colors the expression of the other ideologies.

No one can measure the humiliation of the African under the accepted pattern of relationships once the European dominated the scene, nor plumb the resentment that has gradually accumulated over the years. There were so few literary spokesmen, so few chances for political protest. Perhaps Laurens Van der Post is right when he suggests it can best be discerned by the look of the eye. However, the attitude of the white overlords is stamped in the public record for all the world to see. That venerable servant of Africa, Albert Schweitzer, describes it as follows:

Ever since the world's far-off lands were discovered, what has been the conduct of the white peoples to the coloured ones? What is the meaning of the simple fact that this and that people has died out, that others are dying out, and that the condition of others is getting worse and worse as a result of their discovery by men who professed to be followers of Jesus? Who can describe the injustice and the cruelties that in the course of centuries they have suffered at the hands of Europeans? Who can measure the misery produced among them by the fiery drinks and hideous diseases that we have taken to them? If a record could be compiled of all that has happened between the white

95

and the coloured races, it would make a book . . . which the reader would have to turn over unread, because its contents would be too horrible.[1]

We need not reach back into nineteenth-century colonialism to document it; it is very much alive still. Stuart Cloete and Sir Philip Mitchell are among its foremost contemporary spokesmen in spite of the fact that both are long-term students and public servants of Africa. Cloete in the book, *The African Giant*, paints the African as horrible: "The African has been conditioned by centuries of savage competitive life to seize what he desires wherever he can find it."[2] Sir Philip, writing in the authoritative American study, *Africa Today*, makes the sweeping generalization that Africans are no more than children, members of the only race which has contributed nothing to humanity.

If one finds this attitude in the front-rank westerners in Africa, what can be expected from the rank and file? The following is unfortunately a sampling of the latter: "The African, a child of nature, emerges only to become spoiled and degenerate. . . . He is vicious, unreliable and immoral in all the worst possible ways. . . . He is lazy, shiftless, and lacking in initiative and ambition, and can in no wise adapt himself to machine tempo and western ways. . . . You cannot trust him with positions of responsibility and leadership. . . . Even when removed from his debilitating surroundings and given the chance of living under utterly different and wholesome conditions, on his return to native soil he soon reverts . . ."

Remarks such as these are not rescued from the dim, distant past of the white man's encounter with Africans; they are contemporary. Nor are they restricted to just South African whites, because there are many in South Africa who have progressed beyond this level. Such remarks as these the author heard all over Africa, from British, French, and Portuguese. Consistently derogatory if a bundle of contradictions and falsehoods, they are exactly the soil in which racism breeds, whether in Kenya or Mississippi. They serve to illustrate how serious is the problem the white man has created, mostly by himself, in his dealings with Africans.

At least the Afrikaner of South Africa is honest, if less delicate, in bluntly labeling all the privileges of his society for "blankes" (whites) instead of "for Europeans only." The label "European" is so much more subject to dispute. Is it not possible for an African to become Europeanized? Or perhaps he prefers to become Africanized and still have the privileges of a human being! In either case he becomes a threat to the European hoarding his privileged status. Variations on this problem run throughout the colonies. The French theoretically allow him to enter freely their "civilized" ranks. The Belgians had stages. An "évolué" was an African moving toward Europeanization. In times past he might *de facto* have become a "matriculé," receiving a certificate of merit for having arrived! At the moment both terms are in disrepute. The British operating on their time-honored theory that "it takes three generations to make a gentleman" are equally slow to grant European status to an African, but it can be said that their position has permitted them to make bishops of certain Africans and to knight others. But theirs is a slow process. Most of them working closest with the African in his betterment will concede status to only a few. Apparently it never occurs to them to screen the Britishers who cover Africa to see how many of them have become gentlemen in twenty generations.

In the light of the foregoing, the self-introduction by an African from South Africa at a world conference—"I am a noneuropean, from a non-european country"—scored his point. "European" is not only an elusive label, but an abusive one for all who are not included. For instance, a prominent American Negro travels throughout Africa listing himself on his entrance visas into each country as a "European." And a Japanese nylon salesman may be surprised to find himself, an Asian, also traveling under such visas, but, as one told me, "At the lowest of the European scale." In view of all this, the loud outburst against them in revolutionary Africa should not come as a surprise to westerners. Chief Luthuli told me, "We Africans are prepared to welcome anybody to stay who dissociates himself from foreign fatherlands and who is willing to call himself *African.*" In that he is more generous than most other African leaders.

What so offends the African? What causes these emotional outbursts? Only a non-African raises the question, because in the experience of the African it is an open sore, not once to be forgotten, an ever-present daily humiliation. He does not have to go back into history to uncover the raw scars of ruthless conquest, enslavement, and oppression in order to nurse his resentment and hatred. These raw sores are present, still unhealed, still festering, forever crippling the social body. None can forget slavery, which has been called "the greatest prolonged example in history of man's inhumanity to man." Nor the massacres in the native wars where the superiority in arms wiped out masses of opposition after the fashion of American decimation of the Indians. Nor irresponsible colonialism in the manner of Belgium's King Leopold II. For him Africans existed to be exploited. The stories of baskets of hands, salted and smoked to preserve them in the dank climate, which were brought in from the bush by Leopold's labor-gang bosses shocked even international opinion at the height of the colonial epoch (1908). This horror was immortalized by Vachel Lindsay in "The Congo":

> Listen to the yell of Leopold's ghost
> Burning in Hell for his hand-maimed host.
> Hear how the demons chuckle and yell
> Cutting his hands off, down in Hell.

No matter how exaggerated, these are inescapable elements in the collective memory of Africans.

But it is the present manifestations of racism affecting every single African that rancors the heart of Africa. No list can complete them nor put them in order of priority of offense, but as a sympathetic outsider listening to their endless stories of abuse, I will try in what follows.

Bias Against African Culture. First, there is the slur, explicit or implicit, in most European comments on African society. What is worse, the pretensions of superior culture are made in such a way as to seem to rest in the accident of white skin. Unquestionably the Europeans of South Africa, Central Africa, and East Africa are found doing this most often. The late Prime Minister Malan's position is standard for most whites:

The deeply rooted color-consciousness of the white South Africans arises from the fundamental difference between the two groups. The difference in color is only the physical manifestation of the contrasting irreconcilable ways of life, between barbarism and civilization, heathendom and Christianity.

The overworked term, "white western Christian civilization," has become the loose cover-all for white supremacy, crude and simple. Opposed to this mythical entity is "the backward native," "the black savage," the "barbarian," the "primitive," the "heathen," "the pagan." The blanket label that indicts the whole people of Africa is "the Dark Continent." Almost no attempt is made to appreciate the obvious survival value of the African tribal culture (which to say the least has outlasted western civilization and may indeed survive its collapse), or the cultural assets of the tribal community, or the individual personal differences and achievements of certain Africans. Neither the African society nor the African individual is looked upon as a fact, a value, a thing in itself, intrinsically good. Either he is something to be used and exploited, or a necessary evil around the white man's economic neck, or an object of contempt and disgust. The African is a negative force in the presence of the positive European society, and the contemptuous usage of the terms "pagan," "heathen," and "native" symbolizes his lowliness. "Half-child, half-savage" . . . "lesser breeds without the law." . . . These accusations by the poet laureate of colonialism still hold for many. And should a particular "softhearted," "humane," or "liberal" "kaffir-boetie" ("nigger-lover") pursue a different attitude toward the African, his compatriots quickly try to slap him back into line. A highly sensitive Hollander, recent immigrant to Africa, told of stretching out her hand upon greeting an African, in the presence of her longer settled friends. "Oh, no! You'll have to understand that is not done here," they quickly intervened. The one fact that strikes the outsider is the utter unapologetic way derogatory labels are used without the slightest appearance of viciousness. It is *assumed* that everyone will agree. It is assumed not only by politicians, industrialists, educators, but even by missionaries and dear old ladies knitting in their rockers. They are horrified to have their hands called on the questionable use of these labels—as I discovered to my social embarrassment on several occasions.

When the problem is summed up, as in the following words I heard from one European settler, everyone is supposed not only to sympathize with the plight of the poor outnumbered white on his civilized perch but also to agree with his racist extremes: "You know the relative numbers of black and white in South Africa. Well, consider the black people as a big man struggling in a swamp, and the white people as a little man standing on the edge of the swamp. The little man wants to help the big man. But how far dare he? Isn't it more possible that the big man will pull in the little man than that the little man will pull out the big man?"

The more extreme position is not unlike these words of the late Afrikaner poet, Totius, given in a lecture in 1944 on the subject, "The Policy of the Afrikaners and Scripture."

In Africa, our black part of the world, the most general barbarianism has reached its highest triumph. Africa is a black marsh. How much civilization has been swallowed in the marsh of Africa! The light has tried to infiltrate Africa from the north. It has always died. The same applies to Christianity, but to little avail. . . . The natives differ from all other nations. Blacks and Whites differ so much that a marriage between a Black and a White is unnatural and against the will of God. Therefore we honor our forebears who avoided this abomination. Thus they prevented us from gradually sinking in a black marsh. Thus the will of God with our nation has been fulfilled. Let us be thankful that

God awakened this intuitive insight in the hearts of our fathers, or else the Whites would have disappeared and the Natives would have gained nothing.[3]

Interviewing his son, Professor S. du Tout, in his office at the Theology School of Potchefstroom University in 1959, I learned his claim that this instinctive revulsion had grown out of his forebears' observation of the degeneration resulting from miscegenation. "It was the result of a strong racial consciousness and a feeling of the necessity to keep their blood pure in the same way as they did not expose a pedigree animal to the danger of degeneration which is the consequence of contact with a lower race."

Is it any wonder that someone has remarked that the hardest cross the African has to bear is the attitude of the Europeans toward him? The nineteenth-century, pre-anthropology, naïve view of the supremacy of European civilization still prevails. Is it not known that the white northern European had without challenge evolved to the top of the ladder of history—as God himself had preordained? From a South African paper, August 1959, I copied the following lines:

Christianity has depended all along upon the White man for its existence, its propagation and its survival—indeed upon the White man entirely. . . . Without the survival of the European race, Christianity would go out like a candle. . . . It was the White man who received and followed Christ and who spread his message and made Europe the motherland of Christianity. . . . It has been the White man who has maintained Christianity as the White man's religion whereas after two thousand years, Christianity among the colored and black peoples remains the religion of a small minority, planted there, and only maintained there, by the White man.[4]

Such an attitude hurts the African probably more than the deprivation of social intercourse. His self-esteem is wounded by his being reminded at every juncture that in no circumstance can he be accepted in the white community. The ultimate tragedy is that "For Whites Only" appears not on park benches alone but also on the church pews.

How does the African react to this? We get a clue from the following writer:

Terrified and encouraged, praised and abused, defended and condemned, relegated to the category of "primitivism" and lauded as the seat of civilization, Africa finds herself, in the galvanizing shock of favor and hate, confused. Nobody understands her. Nobody lets her alone. Nobody cares for her. Nobody spares her.[5]

Social Caste System. Coupled to this climate of spiritual—yes, spiritual—contempt is the actual caste status of the African caught in the underpinnings of the European society planted in his homeland. The unhidden purpose of many Europeans is white supremacy, to make European culture completely dominant. To accomplish this most Europeans live in socially segregated compounds or white real-estate reserves. Sir Francis, returning from his chairmanship of the All-Africa Church Committee in the Central Federation, reported what he saw in the *Lagos Daily Times* (October 22, 1959):

Every form of development is planned mainly for the benefit of the European population. On the one hand, you see a happy, free, contented people—riding in cars and owning property, both rich and extensive. This is the white man—self-confident, arrogant and the monarch of all he surveys. On the other hand, you see my people, the Africans, unhappy, subjected, poor, without land and without property worth speaking about. If he cannot cycle, then he must walk. If he has political rights, I did not see any. White and black are poles apart.

Compulsory and voluntary segregation on the part of the dominant power group explains his up-to-date picture. Part of this may be explainable in terms of the need for hygiene, cultural affinity, and sometimes for business, educational, and governmental reasons. But when it becomes the rule of thumb, with the few persons who break with it being scorned, and where its avowed purpose is to keep the European culture sacrosanct and to guarantee its perpetual dominance, it is, to say the least, blameworthy.

The compounds that result are like ice floes in a sea of dangerous waters. Here the entire meaningful life of the average European is conducted. He moves from post office to shops to government houses, to sports and an endless round of lawn parties, and sometimes to church. Always he stays on his ice floe. Nothing occurs outside this round of life except where his duties force him or except for an occasional sporting, fun-making lark to "the disgusting spectacle of native foolishness." If he leaves his own compound he can leap like a seven-league-booted giant to the neighboring European compound. They are so spaced that it is possible for a person to travel from one end of Africa to the other without leaving the sanctuary of these compounds, and as a consequence without seeing anything of the variety and beauty of real Africa, other than this monotonous, cheap imitation of "class" back home.

Trevor and Grace Shaw, that pair of incisive and daring journalists who went into the Congo on a new venture in Christian journalism, using African staff and ideas, told me how even the missionaries were cursed by this self-imposed segregation. They have written about this attitude in their book, *Through Ebony Eyes* (London: Lutterworth Press, 1956):

It is possible to travel through vast missionary territories and yet miss the heart-beat of Africa. It is possible to be so well cared for and so graciously attended by one's missionary hosts, as never to find oneself alone with African blood. It is possible to return at journey's end never having had an opportunity of sitting at the feet of African brotherhood and leadership; never having heard uninterrupted, while night's shadows dimmed one's foreign obtrusiveness, the outpourings of black emotion, and unsurpassable spiritual devotion. It is possible to have seen through one's own eyes, to have seen through the eyes of European colleagues, but never to have seen through ebony eyes.[6]

Is it any wonder that Christianity is looked upon by many as a "foreign faith"? And if that is the picture from the inside, what must it appear to the African who is carefully contained on the outside? Africa has a caste system if one ever existed on this globe. The Europeans' islands are carefully segregated and the African enters them seldom if ever on equal standards, always as a servant, a "boy," an untouchable. All contacts are carefully controlled by the master-servant relationship. It is not surprising that a leading African has said, "In Africa human relations are nearly everywhere reflections of a master-servant relationship in which the sole determinant of who is master and who is servant is the fact of color." I remember with what evangelizing zeal a headmaster of a first-class English prep school in South Africa addressed me at the luncheon to which he had specially invited me to break the good news: "I went to Caux, Switzerland, and now am a confirmed believer in Moral Re-Armament. And there Peter Howard gave me the secret which will cure our South African race crisis." Before I could butt in to ask about this miracle drug, he eagerly told me: "All we have to do is to drop at once and entirely the master-servant relationship." Just that simple. And if simple solutions would work this late in history, the Moral Re-Armament person-to-person simplicity might!

To change the analogy, the social situation may be compared to a feudal castle with the whites being the privileged lords and ladies, and the blacks being serfs who cross the drawbridge only on certain days and to perform certain menial tasks. (Only once or twice did I eat in a white home where the lady of the house cooked the meal, and a missionary assigned within the past year to one of the largest groups of American Protestants covering Africa confided that the examining psychiatrist of his home office insisted that a major mark of his "social sanity" was to conform to the prevailing European pattern of having somebody besides his wife scrub the floors!) In any case the analogy of the drawbridge appealed to one African. He told how a leading churchman had suggested the need for "building bridges" between the two races. "By all means," was the African's reply, "but let us make sure that this time they will not be drawbridges as you have built them in the past, with you controlling them from the inside and allowing us to cross over only at your convenience and when you can use us for your ulterior purposes."

The African has no trouble feeling himself restricted in his social life on every hand. In Africa south of the Congo what we know as "Jim Crow" laws hem him in on every side. The careful student of Africa will know them already: the nuisance laws (curfews, passbooks, police checks, etc.); the total transplanting of millions of persons to locations and Bantustans; the mass separation of manpower from their families and communities to live in the "hygienic hells" (George Orwell) of the labor compounds; the job reservations that preserve the best jobs for the whites; the constant surveillance of police on all the activities of leading non-Europeans. Yes, these are the "bad" that every day strike the eye of the outsider, but can we imagine how the victim enmeshed in the caste system must chafe?

Non-African Control of Africa. The third concrete complaint rests in the fact that the white man who makes up but 2 per cent of the population of Africa controlled until recently 90 per cent of the wealth of Africa. On every hand one hears the complaints: "The white devils stole our land." "The white minority maintain absolute control over the black majority." "First we had the land and they had the Bible; now they have the land and we are left holding the Bible." The barb of these charges rests in the fact that outsiders *do* control the land and the power of most of Africa. We have only to glance at a breakdown of the ratio of the blacks and whites: In South Africa there are 4 nonwhites to 1 white; Southern Rhodesia 10 to 1; Northern Rhodesia 40 to 1; Kenya 130 to 1; Belgian Congo 145 to 1; and in Uganda 700 to 1. Yet the European ruled and got rich.

In the past, the European began his skirmishes in Africa, not often as a friend, but as a predatory enemy—in the slave trade or in the slick deals securing ivory and gold, or in the seizure of vast tracts of African land. No arguments that these were fair-trade deals, understood by both parties, will ever convince the aroused present-day African. For even today, the absolute control of the law and of justice in the hands of the occupying whites, the slight concessions toward representative government nonetheless with widespread taxation, the raping of land and labor resources for the benefit of nations over-the-seas, the broken promises, the armed control that virtually amounts to a police state, and the mass arrests and imprisonment without trial: these are the accumulating present-day charges superimposed on the unpleasant memories of the cruel past. No wonder the "scramble" for Africa on the part of the world's colonial powers has been replaced by the "scram" from Africa on the part of black nationalists. The argument sometimes arises within Africa over whether African nationalism is but hatred for the whites. No wonder the white overlords cherish such misgivings. While it is to be admitted that the injustice is not all on one side—Africans must admit to broken promises, cheating, and irresponsibility on their part—before the justice bar of the world it is not a guess who would win the case.

Yet there are Europeans, beneficiaries of colonialism, living in Africa, who cannot see the error of their ways. I recall with what surprise I was greeted by my host one evening after I had delivered a lecture to an all-African audience on the responsibilities of Freedom Road after the shackles of imperialism have been cast aside. "You don't honestly believe, do you," she pressed me, "that there were actual cases of injustice in the British administration of colonial justice?" She could acknowledge the questionableness of colonialism itself, but she could not bring herself to see that the one-sidedness of absolute power in the hands of a self-interested white minority, no matter how benevolent, inevitably tipped the scales of justice.

The new African speaks confidently, like Mboya when he says, "I reject multiracialism as a solution because I reject everything short of full democracy founded on the equality of individuals." Sir John Moffat, that sage elder statesman of the Federation who tried to prepare for the future with his doctrine of partnership, expresses the misgivings of the whites: "The blacks are becoming more impatient, the whites more scared, the mutual mistrust goes on increasing. And unless there is a sudden outbreak of statesmanship, we are going to have violence."

If violence erupts it will be largely due to the fulfillment of Alan Paton's prophecy that the black man may learn to hate before the white man learns to love. So far, Black protest—the other name for racism in reverse, black supremacy—has figured very little in African affairs. From all over Africa, responsible leadership has repeatedly rejected it. President Nkrumah of Ghana has declared, "I stand for no racialism, no discrimination against any race or individual." The Nigerian lawyer, 'Bola Ige, wrote recently, "We may have been victims of white racialists, but we cannot afford to be racialists ourselves." Kenneth Kaunda, the most likely prospect for the premiership of Northern Rhodesia, told me in our home on the occasion of one of his visits to America, "I refuse to believe that what the white man does against me and my people is done because he is wicked. The white man is only bad because the system is bad. The answer is to change the system. Transfer the power gracefully from the minority to the majority and the whites need not fear anything from the blacks." Sithole summarizes perhaps what is the best judgment of most Africans: "The African hates European domination but does not hate the white man. He welcomes him. The physical presence of the white man in Africa is welcome, but his domination is unwelcome."

Nonetheless, with the world-wide demonstrations over the murder of Lumumba and the affixing of the blame for the interruption of the 1961 U. N. session upon the Black Moslems among the American Negroes, plus the reports of periodic retaliations against the whites in independent Congo, the fear of Black protest is abroad. Louis Lomax, the American Negro journalist who wrote his impressions of contemporary Africa in the book, *The Reluctant African* (New York: Harper, 1960), cites it as the major consideration. In Europe, it may be said that the fear is even greater. Both General de Gaulle of France and the theologian Martin Niemöller of Germany predict a color-war in which the whites would be on the defensive. Stuart Cloete, the

Britisher who specializes on Africa, has said the following differently in many of his writings: "But let us have no illusions. The
black man hates the white. Above all he hates him for being
white, because this is something he can never be."

However, in spite of their testimony and spasmodic evidence
from here and there over Africa, I would not build too much on
this theory. For part of it springs from an exaggerated sense of
guilt for their own share in the white supremacy that has shaped
the presently disturbed Africa. It is true that the white man
largely created the myth in his own mind, and now that the tide
of history is turning he unduly fears receiving back the opposite
number of the monster he created. Or, to put it differently, the
harder you press down a coiled spring, the bigger the kick it
gives back when released. In this sense there is a real danger of
racism in reverse in present-day Africa. Also, as we observe
throughout this book, there have been all along rumblings of
this rising revolt. Perhaps the Kenya leader, Jomo Kenyatta, expresses it best: "A white man will always seek power over the
black man. It is his nature."

The mania of New Africa is not so much Black protest, but
the assertion of "things African" and the mobilization of a
nationalism that pushes the white man into the background. I
was told everywhere that "Africa is no more listening to the
white man." The Africans who thrived by kowtowing to the
white man are being pushed aside by Africans who do not respect "white" just because it is white. The new ones speak of
the latter half of the twentieth century as the "de-mythification"
of the white man in Africa. While the majority of Africans may
still acknowledge the myth of white domination, the doubt has
been planted in the minds of all, and the new African leader has
no patience with it. This should not be begrudged by calling it
Black protest, but should be recognized as a healthy sign of
cultural maturity.

Condescension and Paternalism in Charity. We ought not to
allow ourselves to fall into the trap of seeing no good in colonialism. On the other hand, we ought to see it from the African's

point of view, which meant that even the best deeds were always discolored by a built-in condescension and paternalism. The good will and conscientiousness of the white colonial toward the black African was often carefully clothed in such terms as "white man's burden," "trusteeship," and lately "partnership." At its best it adopted what Albert Schweitzer has declared as his formula with regard to the black man: "I am your brother, it is true, but your elder brother." That may have worked amicably in the nineteenth century, but the younger brother is now a hundred years old and he is more than a little tired of being reminded of the virtues and prerogatives of his older brother.

Paternalism by the European is in the end about as convincing as the allegations of devotion on the part of a lover who simultaneously urges his beloved to marry and live with someone else. This weakness is transparent in such a policy as "separate development" where it is paradoxically claimed that the African's greatest upliftedness comes from contact with the European but the African's best future lies in absolute separation. European paternalism makes no apologies for its blunt policy: "After all, I know and can do more for you than you can do for yourself. That in itself gives me the right to determine your destiny." Consequently, the phrase was coined: "With you, above you, without you." In actual practice the person on the bottom soon learned to tell which part of the slogan took priority. It recalls the story of the husband arraigned for beating his wife with a metal coat hanger. "But," remonstrated the husband, "I thought the Bible said, 'Spare the rod and spoil the child.' " What the judge wanted to know was, "Just when did your wife become your child?" Parenthood is necessary, and paternalism has its benefits, but for a permanent method of good human relations it is questionable.

Africa Without Africans. Finally, there is the grievance about the highhandedness of international conferences where the black man has been involved. Africans have been virtually ignored, not only in decisions affecting the balance of power in the world but also in matters affecting themselves. The power nations of the world have tended to treat Africa as they did at the Berlin Conference of 1884 when they sat at a table without a single African present and sliced up Africa like pieces of pie. Subsequent events have followed suit: the reapportionment of territories following World War I, the use of African men and bases to fight Hitler, the impotence of the United Nations in the face of South Africa's apartheid and her virtual seizure of the Southwest territory, and the need for impartial investigations in such crises as Nyasaland, Congo, Angola, and Cameroons. Worse than these, perhaps, is France's insistence on using the Sahara as an atom bomb test site. The whole western world stands by while a few persons, mostly Africans, protest. (Both ominous and ironical so far as Christianity is concerned is the fact that gatherings of Moslems prayed against this act of "the Christian West"!) The African is expected to fight the wars of the West, to provide boundless resources and bases for these wars, but when Hitlerian tactics are practiced against them they have little recourse.

Is it unfair to claim that Africa has been treated like the back field of the world? We know how the old farmer tries never to think of the back field, uncultivated and lying out; it always reminds him of more hard work. Nonetheless when he has any meanness to do, he retires to the back field. Or when he needs something quickly he gets it without worrying about the aftermath. However, of late he is greatly agitated by the back field. Real estate agents have their eyes on it and by developing all around it they are putting the old farmer on the spot. He must decide what to do with the back field. For the modern West, Africa, that old back field of the world, is coming to the foreground in the developmental schemes of the world's real-estate developers. The old attitudes must give rise to new, especially where Christianity has been too much identified as a western religion.

Now we come to the main burden of this chapter: *What effect do these racial animosities have upon the introduction of Christianity to Africa?* There are some who argue that the primacy of the spiritual in the Christian religion is such that the acceptance

of its truth does not depend upon the purity of its practice. For
such believers the clinching argument is the fact that so many
Africans have become Christians in spite of the known bigotry
and exploitation. Others maintain just as strongly that the acceptance and deep-rootedness of Christianity is in direct ratio to
the sincerity and practice of the missionaries and foreigners who
introduce it. Where the African sees the obvious contradictions
between what the missionary *says* and what both the missionary
and the people sending him *do,* he is disillusioned. For that reason we may speak of the four Christianities the African en-
counters: the Christianity of the primary sources, the Christianity of the missionary, that of the white man in Africa, and that
which the African confronts when he visits a so-called Christian
nation. As he moves from the primary sources, the African becomes more and more disillusioned. This reaction has come to be
called "the missionary boomerang."

In order to get to the bottom of this mix-up we should listen
to the African himself. In letting the African speak for himself
we will be wise to listen to the friends of Christianity as well as
the irresponsible critics. There are plenty of the latter, as is evi-
denced by the following disparaging remarks made against missionaries by Rhodesian speakers at their 1958 African National
Congress. Some of their charges read:

Church funds buy European missionaries fine cars, while African
ministers travel on cycles.

All ministers of religion are thieves. In the Bible nothing is said
about collecting money from Church followers, but these ministers
collect from young and old.

When missionaries are praying they make people look up to Heaven,
and the reason they look down to the ground is because they covet
the land. That is what they are thinking of all the time—giving you
Heaven while they take the land.

But let us hear instead the frank disclosures of the friends of
Christianity, those Africans who not only have benefited from
missions but who have also participated in missions and are cur-

rently leaders in the indigenous church life. Foremost among these is Sir Francis Ibiam, who all his life has been intimately associated with the mission church at all levels, having returned to Nigeria as a missionary doctor and presently heading the famed Hope Waddell School. In the following article *(Social Progress,* April 1960) he pulls no punches:

And so it has been that for generations the black man has been the footstool and the doormat of the rest of the world. His continent was the property of everyone. Intellectually, he had been branded a nitwit. Some European nations believed, and some still believe, that the black man was specially made by God for the benefit of the white man and must remain forever hewers of wood and drawers of water. . . . This kind of treatment breeds hatred and fierce nationalism. It antagonizes Christian evangelism. Let the church ponder over these abnormal happenings in our day and generation. Until Africa and its peoples are received by the church and by the world with open arms, and on equal terms, Christian evangelism in Africa will continue to have a rough passage.

Matching his straightforwardness is this word from perhaps the leading churchwoman of Africa, who together with her husband, Dr. John Karefa-Smart, Minister of Lands, Mines, and Labor in Sierre Leone, wrote in their book on Christianity in Africa, called *The Halting Kingdom* (1959):

Simply increasing the number of church schools, hospitals, and even church buildings cannot by itself outweigh the growing burden of humiliation, distrust, and dislike on the part of Africans, and of arrogance, disdain for things African, and specious paternalism on the part of some non-African missionaries and lay Christians. . . .

African Christians acknowledge and give thanks for these fruits of Western civilization, but many also hold in their hearts the pain and the wounds of a people who, as a race, are generally relegated to positions of subservience in the outer courts, even in the halls of the King who is also their Father and to whom the fellowship has not yet been made real. . . .

There is no longer room or justification in Africa for tribal or colonial or racial churches.[7]

Dr. H. Makulu, in the employment of the World Council of Christian Education and located at the new ecumenical center in Mindola, Northern Rhodesia, told a conference how he suggested that a student read some of the World Christian Book series. "Christianity is a white man's weapon," was the retort. "It is used to weaken the African, but now we have a new weapon to fight them; we have discovered politics!"

As was said earlier, this note of disillusionment is being heard wherever African Christians are given a chance to talk back. The most outstanding job in intergroup communication is being done by the conferences set up all over Africa by the World Council of Churches. A report on their Mindola (Northern Rhodesia, 1958) study group reads:

> The African members—I may say all of them—stressed the point that in the first encounter with Christianity the African soul gave itself in full confidence to the proclaimers of the gospel in whom they saw and also experienced often real saints. (Has ever a people or a group of tribes given themselves with more confidence in the hand of the servants of the gospel? The missionaries were for us as Christ! said one of our members.) Then came after the years the big disillusion that the Church in the complexity of the changing society had great inner weaknesses and did not produce the power to counterbalance the forces of the secular world. At the same time they found that the European part of the Church was inclined to a practically unlimited adjustment to the ideologies and the interests of the European society as a whole. . . . This adagio in different variations we heard in very many of our sessions.

But in spite of the fact that the above comments are rendered by the friends of Christianity, the reader may still have his doubts. In actual practice, is the foreignness, the separateness, the haughtiness of Christianity in Africa as forceful as these Africans report? Are these reports the natural exaggerations of the more sensitive souls? Reporting on the scene as I saw it in 1959 and 1961 all I can do is bring alive the spot-checks that I made on this problem. Let us sample some of the reactions that I personally encountered in different parts of Africa.

From the Congo comes the reaction of a missionary couple who are as close to the thinking Africans as anyone I encountered: "We are shocked to hear some of the bitter prejudice that comes from Africa's lips against the modern missionary movement." In South Africa I was introduced to a young missionary couple just out of Yale and now under the American Board. Their impression was that "the Christian Church for the African cannot be a secondhand imitation, but to discern the truly African elements on which to build is almost impossible for the outsider. The temptation to imitate is great, but the less creative way usually fails to become a vital force in the lives of the people. 'White man's church' is an expression Africans sometimes use for mission churches to indicate their feelings. African sect groups which have few if any vestiges of Christianity about them are flourishing while the Christian evangelization of the African comes forward at a discouraging pace."

In Salisbury, Southern Rhodesia, are several journalists who are still friendly to the Christian cause. One night after supper, to which several of them had been invited to talk over this problem with me, they laid bare their complaints: "Christ made us all brothers, the missionaries tell us. The Bible says so. But politicians and businessmen and a lot of other Christians don't show that they know this. In early days Africans accepted all Europeans without suspicion, for we thought, of course all Europeans are Christian and good. Now we know better. But what do we do?"

In Nigeria, I listened one night to the All-Africa Vice-President of the Presbyterian World Alliance report on his trip to its five-year meeting in South America in 1959. Overflowing with the kindness shown him in the financial provisions for his trip, and in the trust placed upon him by his new office, he exuberantly reported, "Why, even the politicians in the lands of the West are Christian." But the keener among his African audience would not let him get by with this oratorical levity. They challenged him on what he meant by "Christian" politicians. They cited him the destruction of war and the rape of occupation that followed the conquest of certain islands in the late Pacific campaign. They told him how the missionaries hated to return to preach the gospel of peace, purity, and integrity, after they had been so shockingly contradicted by the representatives of "Christian lands."

How deep the cleavage between preaching and practice can be is forever etched on my memory by an experience in South Africa. Having published an account of the famous nineteenth-century world evangelist Andrew Murray, I longed to visit his old home and to sit on the porch where so many sermons and devotional books were composed. At the homestead "Clairvaux" overlooking the colorful South African mountains, I pondered his contribution to the World Church, which included the estab-lishment of a mission seminary in that very town. Today it had two divisions, separated by several blocks, where the white mis-sion students and the colored students lived separately but used the same professors, the same lectures, and had access to the same library. They were to go forth to share the gospel with the col-ored peoples of the world, share fields of work together, share membership in the same church body, but while studying for the priesthood they could not eat, play, or study together. Perhaps the romantic vision of the mission field could not stand the bright exposure of the homefront?

Or again I recall the absolute impasse I reached trying to ex-plain to my East Nigerian students how the racists who claim to be Christian support their white supremacy by the Bible. I was hard put to explain it since they knew their Bible as well as I did and equally as well as the persons referred to. When I cited the Old Testament passages, they were enflamed, especially when they caught the impact of the curse upon Canaan to be "hewers of wood and drawers of water." (Only a person who has lived in that part of the world where the women and children endlessly pursue the creative-killing routine of gathering sticks on their heads and going to fetch water sometimes miles away can appre-ciate the response my information triggered.) They could not believe that there were people in the world who could so pervert the Scriptures to justify consigning a massive block of their fellow mankind to such a debilitating life. They saw at once the utter meanness of the white man perverting even the Bible to relegate *all* black men to the lowest rung of humanity. What surprised them most, I think, is the fact that they had read the same passage many times and had completely missed this interpretation, and they just did not want to believe that some whites could *read into* it such viciousness.

Alan Paton may be said to be sent by God as part of that historic chain of lay protest against an ossified Church. As no white person in Africa, Alan Paton feels the dilemma of Christians caught in the mesh of racism, and with his literary genius he has sought to paint the rough edges of this dilemma in the lives of actual people. There is spiritual depth to his writings. But Alan Paton is disgusted. He kept saying to me in our interview, "Why hasn't the Church been active in reconciliation? Where is the Church in this hour of crisis? What can you offer to defend the Church?" He expressed the despair of a drowning man lashing out for any support. This does not mean that he has forsaken the Church, or will abandon her. At the moment he is active on the All-Africa Church Committee which stirs up more hope for Christianity in Africa than any other single factor. Still he cannot understand how the Church has failed so utterly on this major problem facing Africa, yea, the world.

The Church is momentarily a mockery. Prayers in the Church are insincere, preachers are false prophets, the Gospel is ineffectual. Because there is a gulf between the preaching of the responsibility which we as children of God have for one another and the willingness to accept all the privileges of the Whites and to acquiesce in the fact that non-Whites are discriminated against and wronged in every possible way. That cannot be right, before common reason! How can the Church blink at this tragedy?[8]

When I made my pilgrimage to Phoenix, the rural settlement which Gandhi established north of Durban in the edge of the sugar-cane fields where the coolies brought from India were to labor, I talked with his daughter-in-law. We had tea together. Fortunately, Gandhi's grandson was home on vacation from India, and his granddaughter, a sophomore at the University of Natal, was also present. We visited the Gandhi memoirs: the spinning wheel, the hand-operated press that still produces the issues of *Indian Opinion,* the rondevaal where he meditated, the school he started for underprivileged Indian children. When I saw the dilapidated conditions and the remnants of the family about to forsake the mission, I knew I stood at the end of a dream. When I thought how Christians had treated Gandhi's dream, and how they *still* treat his multitudinous kinsmen in the same region, I shivered at the thought of what impression the Mahatma formed of Christianity as a result of his experience in South Africa. Is it possible that Gandhi might have become a Christian if the local Christians had behaved differently towards him?

If we think of Gandhi pioneering a world that can no longer stomach such discrepancies, what must we think of a Christianity still bound by the ghosts of white supremacy? The blunt conclusion, to be kept in mind in all western deliberations about Africa, is that divisions between and within churches on color lines are no longer acceptable. If we need one single bit of evidence, look only to the rapid rise of sectarians in South Africa, where the historical Church is split more than a thousand ways, more so than anywhere else in the world's history. There are many reasons for this bifurcation, but not least among them is the *closed* doors of the historic churches, the churches of western white men which pretend to be the vehicle of the saving gospel.

What is the total effect of all this racist involvement upon the reception of Christianity in Africa? Will it defeat the Christian faith? No one knows. But what we *do* know is that at present the evangelization of Africa is widely hamstrung by this curse—in fact, is at a virtual standstill in terms of population growth. And this is so at the moment Christianity is being seriously challenged by world movements of gigantic proportions.

The Church which goes under the banner "Brothers in Christ, Limited" is not adequate for Africa in her hour of need.

No missionary leader has seen this more clearly than Dr. Max Warren of the Church Missionary Society of England. "The European or American missionary who sets foot in Asia or Africa today does not merely confront a world in the throes of political re-creation. He meets men and women in whose eyes he can distinguish wariness and suspicion and sometimes hate, in whose hospitality and friendship there is often a reserve which seems to rebut his good intentions. He recoils hurt and resentful unless he can understand and, understanding, love."[9]

The unspoken pathos behind that analysis came home to me again and again as I was taken awkwardly into an African home by my overly-generous African friends. Here I was plunked into a chair by a host who as likely as not had never had a white for tea before and without any other formalities it was announced: "Dr. Bryan is from America. He has come to our country to meet Africans. He says he wants to make friends." The African is unused to outsiders wanting to meet him for the simple purpose of friendship. Heretofore the white man has knocked at their door when he wanted something from them: their services, their lands, their antiques, their idols. He always had some trick up his sleeve when he made his appearance at their hut, in their land. Now the African must get used to meeting him on the level, and unfortunately it is going to be as hard for the African to learn this new relationship as it is for the white man. One confided to me on the occasion of such a home visit: "We have become so accustomed to being told that in our culture we have nothing of worth that we subconsciously believe this ourselves. Both we and the world must get used to welcoming people to see our very own contribution to world culture. We are persons worth knowing in our own right."

It is significant that leaders in the World Church are awakening to this new approach. Leaders as divergent as Father Trevor Huddleston and Billy Graham are urging the world to take a new look at Africa. Both these leaders have announced that racism is perhaps the major hindrance of the expansion of Christianity in the world. As the Graham Crusade moved into Africa for the first time, he proclaimed the decisive policy that there would be no discrimination in his campaign. We can but pray that this spirit will trickle down to the local church and community in order that the present walls of partition can be speedily broken down for the Church in Africa.

6

communism

● ● ● ● ● ● ● ● ● ●

The least appealing and relevant of the alternatives before Africa in the past, but perhaps the most urgent and plausible in the immediate future, is communism. Communism as an overt force is at the moment the least influential of the movements considered in this book, but that does not mean that it is no threat. For by its very nature it is capable of the quickest conquest, since it depends largely on subterfuge, infiltration, and a swift *coup d'état.* Today it may seem negligible, tomorrow it may gobble up the continent. What almost happened overnight on the occasion of the Congo independence is a warning.

"In Africa there is a great danger that newly granted independence may turn out to be but a brief interlude between the rule of colonialism and the harsh dictatorship of international communism." That this prophecy of John Foster Dulles just before his death may come true is in the political stars of the 1960's. The Cold War is taking a fresh turn, this time in the direction of Africa. African leadership is apparently not adverse to the new role of being the Cinderella courted by both sides. Until this decade it could be authoritatively affirmed (by all experts) that "there is no organized Communist party in all of Black Africa." Moreover, native leadership denied any connections with it, both officially and personally. There was little indication of serious study of its tactics and few signs of its effect on influential power groups.

Momentarily we may say that the Soviet is alert to the openness of this transitional stage and of the gullibility of the giddy, power-stricken leaders. Speaking on his Paris tour, 1960, Khrushchev spoke of communism as the world gospel: "This is a secular dream—not only for the Whites, but also of the Reds, the Yellows, and the Blacks. There will be a place for each other under the communist flag. And the sooner this will be, the better for all those peoples." This dream he put over against the assumed impasse of the Moslem-Christian bloc.

Whatever was the status of communism in Africa prior to 1960 is pretty well buried in the secret files of the intelligence services of the Soviet and of the western powers. Mostly rumors and counterclaims dominate the press reports and quick journalistic surveys. A search through them reveals only passing remarks and personal opinions. Of course, documentation is available pertaining to the history of the communist activity in South Africa, where the extended trial of those leaders arrested under the Treason Act finally concluded without indictments. And small groups of communists were known to operate in French territories where the party is not banned. Moreover, facts are available with regard to the concrete overtures which the Soviet has made to the newly independent African states. Guinea, Sudan, Egypt, and Ethiopia have all received multimillion-dollar loans. The latter nation, as the oldest of the African states, has had a long history of friendly relations with Russia. Besides receiving benefits, such as the main hospital in the capital city, it has figured in the German-Russian designs of the thirties. Most recently (1959) Khrushchev made a personal gift of the first jet plane to the Emperor. At the beginning of the sixties Premier Toure of Guinea had fallen almost entirely into the Soviet bloc and President Nkrumah of Ghana had opened his country to Soviet economic experts, mainly agricultural. The unsettled conditions of both the Congo and the Cameroons bred communist-led parties. The USSR maintains diplomatic relations with Tunisia, Ghana, Ethiopia, Sudan, Egypt, Guinea, Morocco, and the Congo. Radio Moscow is clearly audible in much of Africa, and at the moment they are expanding the power of their beam to Africa. But perhaps it is through the labor unions, whose leaders are wielding undue strength in the new developments, that the communists have penetrated farthest. The World Federation of Trade Unions has tried to capture the Ghana unionists; in French West Africa there is an affiliate of the communist-dominated CGT (General Confederation of Labor) in France; whereas in fact the Sudan Workers Trade Union Federation is communist-dominated.

But what is known on the surface of communist maneuvering may have little reality compared to the actual impact of infiltration from within. All that is publicly known now is that many African nationalists have been feted in Russia and at international communist affairs. In nearly every free country of Africa there are leaders high in the power struggle who have been recipients of this wooing. As far back as 1928, the Sixth World Congress of Communist International stated the necessity of infiltrating Africa through students. In line with that, colonial students' organizations, such as the World Federation of Democratic Youth (Budapest) and the International Union of Students (Prague), have arisen in recent years. Students have been going to Russia over the past decades, but George Padmore, who was himself one of these privileged and who visited Russia frequently before his defection from communism, concludes that there were never "more than a dozen." A 1960 survey discloses less than 200 African students in training in all Russia, but a counter report puts the figure around five thousand. Recently, in addition to the older Kutvu University, which exists alongside Lenin University for western students and is open to Asian and African students, the Soviet opened an enlarged university for a greater appeal for the latter (promptly dubbed an "apartheid" university by the rest of the world) . In 1961 it reportedly processed 500 acceptances from 35,000 applications.

The summer of 1959 was the occasion of the Vienna Youth Festival, which was followed by a free tour for the African delegates and the red carpet treatment in Russia, the bill being footed by the Soviet Committee of the Afro-Asian Solidarity Conference. Earlier in April there was formed the Soviet Association of Friendship with African Peoples, which included among its listed backers the American Negroes, Shirley Graham (wife of DuBois), Paul Robeson, and Alpheus Hunton, all living in Moscow. While it may be that the fully trained professional and technical student is not yet returning from Russia, the number of those having been there had reached such proportions that in October 1954, the African Ministers of Nigeria in a public policy denounced them and foreclosed the civil service to them. Besides leaders like Toure and Mboya, it is known that others in the Congo and in the Cameroons have trained there.

No question about it, the Soviet is rolling out the red carpet for Africans. The same summer of the Youth Festival, Haile Selassie was feted for fourteen days, at the end of which he was crowned with the award of a Doctorate of Jurisprudence by Moscow University. In the process, he was told by Russian guides, "We have the same religion as Ethiopia" (meaning, no doubt, that the generic ties of Eastern Orthodoxy and the Coptics are closer than those of the latter with the western Church). Since then, Khrushchev has promised a visit to certain African countries. The Russians can be assumed to be present on every side of this seething pot called Africa.

The present fluidity of Africa, with its revolutions, its social vacuum, and its personal ambitions, is a ready-made site for Soviet advances. The new leaders are astutely aware of the cruciality of the role they play in the balance of power between the East and the West, and they are not averse to playing this game to the full, even to the extent of forgetting past indebtedness to the West and of getting trapped in something far worse than western imperialism. The warning with regard to the threat of a new type of colonialism has been sounded wisely by Nkrumah. But the ecstasy of the new leadership courted by the power nations of the world is not likely to be brought to its senses by sober words.

This helps explain why the comments of Africans about communism vacillate between the purely naïve to the shrewdly calculating. Typical of the former is the 1956 press report of an interview with Haile Selassie: "Communism has no hold on my

people at present. But my people understand from listening to
the radio that communism has done a lot of good for certain
countries." Typical of the latter is the "positive neutrality"
policy of most West African nationalists. Dr. Azikiwe, first gov-
ernor-general of free Nigeria and who led the fight for West
African independence with his outspoken chain of newspapers,
admits openly that "We are in a position to wring from the
West just about what we want so long as we play our trump card
('You know we can always invite in Russia') effectively." A
student in Kenya in 1961 boasted of Kenyans' academic excellence as follows: "We now sent the largest number of students to
the University of East Africa, and the largest number to the
States [not factual]. And, I assure you, we shall soon have the
largest delegation enrolled at Moscow's new university." His
naïveté was scarcely worse than President Nkrumah who recently
interpreted his policy of neutrality as needing to send as many
Ghanaians to the East to study as are presently matriculating in
the West (*viz.* 3,000) . The more realistic African leaders do know
that the communists have worked out an effective system of
maintaining high capital formation rates in underdeveloped
areas. Their cult of industrialization, with the blast furnace, the
hydroelectric plant, the bridge, the railroad—all symbols of
gigantic power—makes a quick impact on the man emerging
from bushfarming and straw and mud huts.

However, the common man, the man in the village, is likely to
be even more naïve. Without a sense of twentieth-century world
history, he is without the knowledge either of the blood purges,
the brainwashing, and the new form of imperialism of the
Soviets, or of the economic dialectics that brought communism
into existence. On the other hand, his own tribal background
does not make him as suspicious of communal projects and of the
submergence of the individual into the group as is the individualistic westerner. Typical is the attitude of the magazine vendor
on the ferry I was taking to Calabar. In his arm, along with *The
Reader's Digest, Time,* and some British periodicals, were four
Russian journals. As I recall, one was on Russian football, an-

other on Russian health, another on co-ops, another on art. All were in English, in the best picture-appeal, tabloid format, though obviously stilted and giving the appearance of having been created just for the occasion and not as a regular periodical. Teasing the vendor, I inquired, "How is it that you sell poison along with your medicine?" Finally getting the point, he broke into a broad grin and admitted that he made a hundred per cent profit on each Russia magazine: a shilling on every two shillings' worth, which was twice what he made on his western sales. On further questioning, I became aware that he never read his wares, to make comparative judgments, and perhaps cared little about my insinuation of "poison."

Chief Luthuli, whom I asked about the report of communists within the ranks of the African National Congress which he heads, declared that he had carried on a fight to keep them out, but nevertheless he confessed, "In the struggle for black rights, I am not choosey about my allies. If they want to fight alongside us, on our terms, who am I to stop them?" The general attitude over Africa seems to be that the West is making too great a fuss over communism. For them, the alarm in the West is not justified, and they do not wish to sell out too soon to a conflict in the outer world which may not apply at all to their own situational needs.

One has to admit that there is considerable ground for their logic. As they read the western press, listen to the western radio, and attend western conferences and universities, they hear all too much of "hate communism." Unquestionably they encounter a one-sided approach. Their reaction turns into something like this (as one actually confided to me): "If two people are talking, and in the conversation one party consistently maligns a third person not present, the automatic reaction of the second party is to identify himself with the third party about whom he knows nothing, if for no other reason than that the vehemence of the outbursts and his past experience with the first party leaves him in doubt about the accuracy of his appraisal." Or, as someone from Uganda put it, "The western countries fear communism as some African societies used to fear evil spirits. An African who expresses his mind freely is branded as communist." This unfortunate tendency to identify all protest on the part of Africans against the ruling powers as "communist-inspired" beclouds all future attempts at clarification.

When one adds to that natural psychological reaction the inflammatory factor of color prejudice, then the tendency to identify with the third party (in this case, Soviet communism) is boosted. "Could it be," they frequently ask, "that Americans feel more for their white brothers under the domination of Russian whites than they do for blacks under the domination of Western European whites? You know, it is so easy for the Africans to draw this conclusion." An editorial in the *West African Pilot* (June 30, 1953) puts in capsule form the prevailing attitude of the African with regard to what the West calls "the menace of communism":

We know no more about communism than what its American and British detractors have pushed across to us as propaganda. . . . But judging from what we see and experience from day to day, we feel that all this talk of the so-called "free world" and "iron curtain" is a camouflage to fool and bamboozle colonial peoples. It is part and parcel of power politics into which we refuse to be drawn until we are free to choose which ideology suits us best.

For the time being, we shall judge every nation strictly on the merits of the attitude of the nation toward our national aspirations. We have every cause to be grateful to the communists for their active interest in imperialism. It is then left to the so-called "free nations" to convince us that they are more concerned about our welfare than the communists, and in this regard we believe more in action than in mere words.

Moreover, the Africans feel some kinship with communism because of their indigenous background of tribalism, and also from the introduction of idealistic biblical and humanistic utopianism. Considering the latter first, we may say that there is plenty of communistic thinking in Africa, communism tinged with Marxism but getting its main thrust from the Bible and

Fabianism. Little orthodox communism—of the hard-hitting logic of a Lenin or of the brutal tactics of a Stalin—exists. Consequently, Nkrumah astonishes the world by calling himself "a Christian socialist" and by speaking of his purposes as prime minister as "merely aiming to put the Sermon on the Mount into my government." If outsiders are tempted to ridicule this religious idealism as pure bosh, then some thought should be given to the role of the Orthodox kibbutzim in Israel, or of the duration of such religious social experiments as the Society of Friends, the Mennonites, and the Hutterites. What Julius Nyerere labels the communitarian ideal—combining the best of tribal communism and of western individualism—has a concrete appeal in Africa.

That this is more than religious dreaming or political propaganda is substantiated by the sound sociological attention which African leaders and their conferences have given to the new society that may emerge. They speak of the possibility that Africa may supply the answer to the world's social pilgrimage. In the lead article in *New York Times Magazine,* March 27, 1960, Tanganyika's foremost politician, Julius Nyerere, put the possibility in persuasive terms: "Having come into contact with a civilization which has overemphasized the freedom of the individual, we are in fact faced with one of the big problems of Africa in the modern world. Our problem is just this: how to get the benefits of European society—benefits that have been brought about by an organization based upon the individual— and yet retain Africa's own structure of society in which the individual is a member of a kind of fellowship. . . . The African is not 'communistic' in his thinking; he is—if I may coin the expression—'communitary.' "

Communism is no *gospel* (as Khrushchev claims) to the Africans. As has been said, the traditional tribal system "out-communizes" the Soviets. But one must be clear to keep the distinction between *primitive* communism that arises from man's primary relations with nature and *ideological* communism of the Marxists and *technological-state* communism of the Soviet Union and of China. Of the former variety, it may be said that the articulate African is sufficiently acquainted with it, having most likely thrown off its communal ways and its communal mentality, to be aware both of its defects and of its advantages. In that light, the African is more likely to be disillusioned with "the gospel of communism," as it issues from Europe (since he identifies Russia with the West, and with the devastating imperialism of the western world), than is the westerner who merely reads about the perils. The new African has just now disentangled himself from his animistic tribalism; he is not ready to submerge himself again so soon. The new African is just now casting aside the shackles of imperialism; he is not ready to welcome the white European with another form. Moreover, he is keen enough to see that the strong kinship system provides communal benefits which no government can impose from above. Finally, his new loyalties, whether the faith of Islam, Christianity, or nationalism, furnish substitute allegiances.

We will speak later of the assistance that Islam and Christianity give for the African's rejection of communism. Momentarily, nationalism in its most rabid form is perhaps Africa's best bulwark against communism. That great architect of African nationalism, George Padmore, whose premature death in 1959 cut short his promising guidance for the new Africa, courted Russian communism much of his life, but in the end exposed it relentlessly. "The only force capable of containing Communism in . . . Africa is dynamic nationalism based upon a socialist programme of industrialization and co-operative methods of agricultural production. . . . Africans only lend ear to Communist propaganda when they feel betrayed and frustrated; when they have lost hope in the professions and promises of Western so-called Christians, who, while paying lip service to 'the brotherhood of man', perpetuate the 'exploitation of man by man', especially coloured man."[1] Padmore strove to place over against the spell of communism the rallying cry of "Pan-Africanism."

We can summarize by listing first the factors which lend themselves to the introduction of communism into Africa, then the factors that militate against it. The following facts, some of which we have observed, appear favorable to communism's growth in Africa:

1. The fluid, even revolutionary, state of the transition from external political control to self-government, where youthful ambitions in the opposing parties may capitalize on the appeal to the communist world bloc.
2. The false identification between the communalism of the tribe with the promises of a politico-technological communism.
3. The returning students thoroughly convinced by the showpieces, the scholarships, and the tours in communist countries.
4. The "positive neutrality" of the new nation-states, which in its attempts to keep the Cold War out of Africa may actually play into the hands of the Soviet, which apparently has high hopes for an African satellite.
5. The rapid industrialization with its rootless workers, the complete displacement of old land ties, and the growing corruption, inefficiency, and resort to police control—all these on the part of the new governments may elicit a "people's movement."

On the contrary, the following facts seem to work against the growth of communism in Africa:

1. The ideological ties with the free and open society of the West run deep in the blood of the African elite, as they have developed their labor unions, their universities, their churches, their press, and their parliamentary democracy. Their non-African mentors, their own personal commitments, and their first institutions are all noncommunist, if not anti-communist.
2. The nationalist leadership at the moment is not proletarian-oriented, nor does it gain power by playing class against class. It is mostly of upper-crust origin and draws its fire principally by yelling "bloody colonialism."
3. The rural conservatism of the predominant agrarian sector, which is still largely "prosperous" and working successfully, serves to reinforce the inherent values of the traditional communal life.
4. Momentarily, virtually all leaders and power groups are on record

as being free of communist members and as being anti-communist in theory and policy.

5. What interest there is in communism as a theory and as a strategy is mostly casual and spasmodic; there is no sustained study or at-attempt to apply it to the African situation, as did Mao in China.

If, as is so often the case with armchair comparisons, this makes it sound as if the coming of communism to Africa is a tossup, then we must be more specific and fair. We must remember that it takes only a sudden, unexpected turn of events to upset the best of rational analyses. Such a turn of events could very well be the rapid rise of a restless and uprooted proletarian segment in the overnight industrialization of Africa, under the new elite. Again, the strong-arm tactics of the personality-cult democracy could provoke the subterranean formation of an opposition party which by using guerrilla methods could overthrow the existing government. Or, a false move on the part of an overprotective western power seeking to continue an unlimited and final say-so in African affairs might turn public opinion toward the East. Africa at the moment is like a spinning top, wound up by the powerful forces of the twentieth century, and nobody is able to predict which way it may fall.

While the West enjoys some advantages at the moment over against the communist challenge, Robert C. Good, co-ordinator of President Kennedy's task force on Africa, has summarized certain serious disadvantages.[2] First, Africa is reacting against western imperialism, not Soviet domination, in the past. Second, the communist countries seem to offer more relevant models for economic development and political integration. Third, there is the psychological manifestation of cutting the apron strings: the new African nation-states seem to think they must oppose the western powers on certain issues to assert their independence. Finally, there is a natural concurrence of interests between the aggressive Africanists and the communists, in that both seek to exploit a fluid situation to move as quickly and as far as possible away from being the back door of Europe to being a new power-bloc in the world. The communists naturally support any move designed to undercut Europe's traditional position and pretend to support enthusiastically the radical regimes of Africa.

The direct intervention of the communist bloc in African affairs is widely known. Her agents, her material assistance, her loans, and her diplomatic offices are not hidden. And her everpresent propaganda in Africa and in the world at large is endlessly exploiting the continent's colonialism, racism, and instability. It is Russia's indirect action that is less known, her hidden methods. Africa being the ripe plum it is, ready for the picking, is bound to invite the best strategy of the communists aiming at nothing short of a decisive victory.

What can stop communism in Africa? Nasser boldly proclaims, from the pinnacle where he eyes the continent with an eagle's care for its prey, that only the Moslem faith can check its avalanche southward. The Moral Re-Armament crowd make claims that they have rescued key leadership from the clutches of the communist evil. In actuality, the United Nations blocked the likelihood of a communist take-over in the Congo, and still delivers the best hope. The Catholic Church launched its counterattack years ago, having the wisdom to see that the coming revolution with its massive unsettlement served to invite communism. It is reliably reported that the Vatican aims to steal the thunder of the communists—"the emancipation of the colored races"—by promoting the formation of African independent states and by moving toward the Africanization of its own church life. Already it has African bishops and a cardinal, and is presently thinking of the canonization of an African saint. It has accelerated its activity in politics by vigorous and successful intervention during elections, by the creation of thinly disguised Catholic parties, and by seizing power more directly. It is rumored in certain West and equatorial African countries that some political parties have made ententes with the Church.

What can be more safely predicted is that if desperation in its many forms—whether born of physical starvation, political rev-

olution, psychological uprootedness, or spiritual meaninglessness
—can be withstood by Africa in the years of its political experi-
mentation and its economic development, then communism may
be thwarted. But who, looking at volatile, juvenile Africa, can
expect a stable teen age?

7

educationalism

● ● ● ● ● ● ● ● ● ● ●

The speed with which higher education has come to Africa and the passion which marks the African desire to secure it justify the treatment of it as an "ism." If we add to that the virtually unquestioned faith in the old H. G. Wells formula— that civilization is a race between education and chaos—then we can understand why education is the rage. The young African, ambitious to become a leader, feels that he must "catch up with the world" in a few short years. What unparalleled opportunities this affords and what dangers lurk alongside this path is seldom appreciated.

In what follows we shall concentrate on the university facilities available for the Black African, mentioning only incidentally those available to the European, as in South Africa, and to the Arab, as in North Africa. First, there is a general survey of these facilities, with some detailed and intimate glances at differing types of campuses, that the reader may get the advantage of the author's visit to all the universities of Africa. Then, there follow some general observations on the over-all pattern and problems of African higher education, with particular reference to the role of religion.

Africa is disturbed by education and disturbed Africa wants education. The proportions of this urge are manifest in the rapid formation of its universities. All nine of the university colleges in Africa south of the Sahara have attained their present status since World War II, most in the past five years. The two in the Congo graduated their first students in 1960. The University of Dakar received its inaugural charter from De Gaulle in December of 1959. Liberia is still a fledgling although it was proclaimed a university in 1951. Of the five in British territories, four are of recent origin: Makerere for East Africa, located in Kampala, Uganda; University of Nigeria at Ibadan; University of Ghana at Achimoto outside Accra; and University College for Central Africa, at Salisbury, Southern Rhodesia. Only Sierre Leone, with its Fourah Bay College, which had existed as a preparatory school since 1816, becoming affiliated with the University of Durham in 1870, and a full-fledged university college in 1960, has a long history. The tenth university college for Africans (there are eight others in the Union of South Africa reserved entirely for Europeans, upon the new ruling effective January, 1960) is in the peculiar position of retrogression. Unquestionably the most influential of all the institutions of higher education among Africans, Ft. Hare has now been reduced by the new policy of the Nationalist government to a tribal college, or to what they call a "Bantustan" branch of their university system.

In a separate category are five other institutions open to Africans. First, located in Basutoland, is Roma, the Roman Catholic College which is pressing for university status. Strategically located in this African-ruled British protectorate, it can provide an integrated model to the strict segregation surrounding it there in the southern region of Africa. Second is the University College of Ethiopia, at the capitol city, Addis Ababa, which is at present staffed mostly by Canadian Jesuits. Third is the up-and-coming campus at Khartoum, formerly Gordon College, but now giving the appearance of being entirely Arabic and Moslem-oriented. Fourth and fifth include the university system of Egypt, composed of the four secular universities and the distinguished historical Moslem Al-Azhar. Together they carry by far the major part of higher education in Africa, the sum of which outdistances the combined work and students in all· the other institutions cited. The four secular universities, including the first-rate University of Cairo, are reported to serve over one hundred thousand students, whereas Al-Azhar, recognized as a university in the thirties, secured a new campus quadrangle in

1950 and today has 5,545 students. Though Moslem, its main support is from the government, and it operated on a six-million-dollar budget in 1959. Also not to be overlooked are the famous American University in Cairo, operated for nearly a century under Protestant missionary direction, and the Karaouine University in Morocco, now in its 1,101st year.

All told this makes a total of twenty institutions of college and university status open to Africans (though of course Europeans are not forbidden). Two facts are noteworthy. One, the number of Black Africans attending these new university centers does not equal the number studying outside the continent. This is explainable partly in terms of the prestige which accompanies study abroad. Nonetheless, the combined figure is still low, abysmally so, an estimated 7,000 students, most of whom are in the United Kingdom, with some 1,700 reported to be taking some form of study in the United States in 1960. Black Africa's own universities have less than five thousand, with the reported number of graduates in 1959 reaching only two hundred. In other words, the whole of Black Africa has a university system producing needed graduates to an extent no larger than a *single* middle-sized university in America! Even so the distribution is most disparate. On the one hand Nigeria could boast of over 22,000 with degrees, while colonial Congo had scarcely a dozen. The contrast is further magnified when we keep in mind the approximately three and one-half million college students in America. (Needless to say, Russia is making its bid, and while the number of Africans who have matriculated there is much lower than hysterical commentators have estimated, they are said to be selecting some 500 from 35,000 applications for scholarships to Moscow's brand-new Friendship University for Africa-Asia.)

The second observation is that the African university system is just now moving into its secular stage. One observes from the facts above that all the older institutions are of religious origin. For instance, the missionary colleges, Fourah Bay, Ft. Hare, and Gordon, have a combined history of over three hundred years. Their Christian background shows up in other ways too, for example, in the layout of the campuses and the traditions. The student residences of the University of Ghana have private chapels, and the University of Nigeria has both Protestant and Catholic chapels of architectural excellence in keeping with the rest of the campus. Louvanium is unforgettable for its massive fish-shaped chapel dominating the campus on the hill outside Leopoldville. Religion is part of the curriculum of most, and three of the universities have developed outstanding departments, with Sierra Leone and Ghana establishing journals of religion within the past three years.

Nonetheless, there is a pronounced secular trend, with departments in the social and technical sciences leading the revolt against the religious and humanities foundations of the schools. What this foreshadows, I am afraid, is contained in Toynbee's prediction that the Afro-Asian nations appear to be swallowing the technological husks of western civilization without digesting the spiritual kernel. This is not to say that the new nation-states do not have a right to develop whatever form of education they want or need. It is rather to fear that in the rush to provide higher education they appear to forget the roots of the plant called "university." For instance, an issue already before one of the new states is the question of the freedom of the university, from which in this particular case emanates most of the opposition to the incumbent government. Can academic freedom and competent research prevail where the university is not buttressed in a philosophy transcendent over pragmatic social needs?

The rush for increased higher education is not conducive to reflection along these lines. Already the new university opened in East Nigeria in 1960, and the prospects of another for Liberia and the first ones in the Ivory Coast and Guinea, promise to follow the secular pattern. As yet there is no immediate hope for Black Africa's *first* independent Protestant college or what is distinguished in America as the privately endowed Christian university. However, the Southern Baptist mission has funds allocated and will proceed to build when and if their Nigerian constituents raise ten per cent of the capital outlay. The Protestant Council in the Congo issued a call for such an institution as long ago as 1952, but the urgency of the Congo crisis ten years later has just now produced the envisioned Congo Technical Institute. In the meantime Roman Catholics are planning two more universities for Black Africa, one in Liberia and one in Nigeria.

Let me return, for the sake of a clearer picture of the new university system of Africa, to a more detailed and intimate picture of campuses representative of several parts of the continent. At all of them the physical layout with the beauty and spaciousness, the architectural accommodation to local forms and climate, and the openness to the African challenge, is enough to arouse the envy of the rest of the academic world. For instance, consider the first French overseas university, located four miles from Dakar on the 173-acre campus fixed on the cliffs of volcanic rock. Its twelve buildings catch the seabreeze of Africa's westernmost point. Its 1,253 students (1958-59) are well cared for, having menus varied for Moslems, Africans, and Europeans. My visit on the occasion of De Gaulle's address in 1959 gave me the impression that it is the most cosmopolitan of all the universities in Africa. Sixty of its students are women, and one of seven are non-African, since it is the first of the African universities to attract local European families. A breakdown of statistics about its student body reveals that 544 study law (which department has trebled in enrollment in the last two years) ; 128 are in medicine, dentistry, and pharmacy; 294 in science; and 287 in arts. Protestants compose only a handful of the students. The world-famous IFAN (*l'Institut Français d'Afrique Noire*) is now relocated on the campus, leaving its renowned museum downtown. Its diversified services to French West Africa include fathering the *Institut des Hautes Etudes* at Abijan, Ivory Coast, which may soon attain its own university status. In buildings adjacent to it are trained administrators, commercial agents, and teachers. There is also the going and coming of many specialists who help the West African governments in their new status as members of the French Overseas Community. Here is no isolated ivory tower, but a relevant institution, mindful of the French culture on the one hand and the "African personality" on the other.

As a second example, let us go to the far east of Africa, to Uganda, where the British established their university college for that vast territory. (Incidentally there is a strong move afoot to make the Nairobi Technical College, which has giant new buildings of the same functional design as the rest of the city in its downtown setting, a second university. The majority of Makerere's male students now originate in Kenya.) In 1959, this institution of parklike grounds on the rolling mountains covered with tropical vegetation and the profuse coloring of flowers on every side, had nearly one thousand students, of whom 68 were women. Women students were first admitted in 1945, when six girls from Uganda entered. This fact is remarkable inasmuch as traditionally African women are brought up to be shy and retiring. But here in the heart of Africa women are coming into their own. However, the significance of the percentage is reduced when one considers that of the 68 women only 40 are African. The rest are Asian, who have a much better financial background and more opportunities for preparatory school.

Speaking further of women, the most study arts; only ten are reading science. Three are studying medicine, seven are in the School of Fine Arts, and ten are advancing in the Department of Education. Looking back over the past fifteen years one learns that Uganda has successively supplied most of the women students. All told, 48 Uganda women have completed courses at Makerere, of whom 30 are teachers. Five have arts degrees. Of the remaining 18, several are working for community development, some are housewives, and one qualified as a doctor of medicine in 1959, thus becoming the first African woman doctor in East Africa. No woman has yet read agriculture or veterinary science. Two women graduates—both married—sit in the Legislative Council, the Parliament of Uganda. I had the privilege of dining with the family of one such graduate. She remarked, as we ate a meal entirely of African cooking, that under the older customs wives were not allowed to eat eggs or poultry, these being reserved for the male. Then she announced pontifically, "This is no longer so in *our* family," as she reached for the second helping of eggs. "Ours is a liberated home."

Although Makerere is open to Europeans there has up to now been only one, a girl from Uganda. Of the two in residence during the year 1959, one is from Kenya, the other from Tanganyika. It may be that as Makerere raises its standards it will attract more, but one cannot help contrasting the virtual absence of Europeans matriculating in this British territory with the large number matriculating in the French and Belgian territories.

We drove out some ten miles southwest of Leopoldville on the Matadi road to get to Louvanium. It lies on an elongated tract of land that, while it is only 500 acres, seems to extend over almost three miles of territory and already has some ten miles of new roads on university land itself. It is perched high above the city of Leopoldville and above the beautiful Congo River. The cost of the initial university buildings has been set at $14,000,000; and the Congo government, which does not do things by halves, has contributed a flat 80% of this. The balance has come from private and corporation gifts of companies like the Union Miniere, and people jokingly say that the energetic rector has gotten 25% from this source, so that he has 105% in all to work with!* The rector, a young atomic scientist, has spent a year of research in atomic laboratories in the U.S.A. and has represented the Belgian government on several commissions. His gifts as a builder and organizer and leader of men have made him almost a legend in Leopoldville, and what he has accomplished in three short years almost took our breath away. Through his good offices, Africa has its first atomic reactor placed there. The university buildings are handsomely built and the student dormitories and refectory, the medical school and the new university hospital, the science laboratories and the classrooms—to say nothing of fifty faculty homes, faculty swimming pool, visitors' lodge, and the rest—show what Belgian genius and adequate resources under-

---

* All these figures apply to the pre-independence period; but significantly it is presently flourishing.

took when they, at what now proves to be a date too tardy, changed their policy.

The plans for the ultimate size of the student body are at present being set at a thousand students and already almost two hundred students are in attendance. One-third of these are white and two-thirds Africans. No African women have as yet enrolled, but there are twelve white women students. When the university opened its doors in 1956, there were 30 Africans and 3 whites who enrolled; the second year there were 80 Africans and 8 whites; the third year there were 110 Africans and 50 whites. In 1959, there were 127 Africans and 108 European students; in 1961 410 students, 340 of whom were Congolese. In the eyes of the Africans, the presence of the whites is a kind of vindication of the quality of the teaching offered. At the time I was there no racial barrier was apparent: white students resided in the same comfortable dormitories and they ate together in the dining hall. The University statement on the matter of race read as follows:

It has been decided from the outset that the Louvanium University should, without any distinction whatsoever, be open to all students who are able and willing to get a university education in the Congo and who respect the spirit of the University and the domestic regulations. The young people from the metropolis share a common life with the native students. Any discrimination within the premises or in the conditions of life is quite out of the question.

It is too bad that both this regulation and the university itself had to come so late in the history of Belgian occupation of the Congo.

A real venture in interracial education occurs in the recently established University of the Rhodesias at Salisbury. In 1960 its first graduates moved into the life of the community, products of a campus where races live, work, and play together. True, during its third year Africans numbered only 33 in a student body of less than 200, and the financial support has been seriously threatened by the reactionary white settlers locally. Moreover, there were not at the time of my visit any Africans on the fifty-five-member teaching staff. Still it is more than encouraging that even where the talk of "partnership" is being challenged by Africans restive because of the few concrete signs of it, students of both races can be together on the same campus with the same professors and the same curriculum.

As can be seen, there is a universality, a cosmopolitanism, about these universities that makes one wake up and stare at this new Africa. Most students are bilingual, even multilingual. The student body contains a wide composition. Faculties are recruited from many countries. Visiting lecturers are supplied by the various countries competing for the affection of Africa. The universities have quickly emerged to become the centers for political agitation, Pan-Africanism, and international conferences. In fact, as one observer puts it, these universities are doing as much as any universities in the world to build international understanding. What follows are two illustrations of his point. Ft. Hare College has as diversified a student body as is found in Africa: Xhosa, Zulu, Swazi, Sotho, Tswana, Indian, Colored, and European. (In fact, some people think this is the basic reason for the government's decision to reduce it to a single ethnic grouping.) The Ethiopian college, under Emperor Haile Selassie's initiative, got the jump on the others in its bid for Pan-Africanism when the Emperor announced at the 1958 All-Africa Peoples' Conference that it was providing fifty scholarships for students anywhere in Africa. Visiting there, I made it my business to meet some of these students who had just enrolled under the program. And flying down east Africa, I later sat alongside such a scholarship student, a girl from Zanzibar. I asked her how it was possible for her to be *flying* home on holiday, several thousand miles. She replied, "Oh, we are treated quite well by the Ethiopian government. All our living expenses and more." More and more this cross-fertilization is occurring at the university level.

Along with this healthy cosmopolitanism, there is a fast-growing intellectual elite, something not altogether beneficial. The premium put upon "the man of ideas," the desire to be a white-collar paper worker, to become "a clerk," is the uglier side of this new environment. Unfortunately it takes bizarre forms, as it so often does among college sophomores in America giddy with their new status. For instance, at the University College of Ibadan the dining hall tables after meals had piles of crust cut from the bread. When I asked about it, I was curtly told that "nobody who is somebody eats bread crusts." But this is the least dangerous of the traits of the pseudo-intellectual. Schweitzer, it will be remembered, encountered the same problem when he asked an African hospital attendant to help move some logs. "I am an intellectual and don't drag wood about." Schweitzer countered with, "You're lucky; I too wanted to be 'an intellectual,' but I didn't succeed." In a similar vein, Robert Gardiner, a Ghanaian now head of the U. N. Economic Aid Office for Africa in Addis Ababa, told how the newly educated young Ethiopians are reluctant to go back into the bush to share their knowledge with their countrymen. There is a touch of historical irony in his rejoinder: "Remember, my fellow African, the British Empire was not built by brave young Englishmen afraid to go to the bush!"

The greatest danger foreseen as a result of this attitude is that the technical knowledge and application needed at this crucial moment of Africa's development will be lacking. Among the several factors that seem to be responsible for this attitude, these three are vital. First of all, the higher education transplanted to Africa tended to be an unimaginative carbon copy of that which the European had had himself. Few adjustments were made, and the ordinary respect shown to a teacher in Europe carried with it in Africa an exaggerated form of authority. The African, being a superb imitator, tends to copy its surface manifestations along with its basic structure, without much discrimination of what should be cast aside and replaced by more genuine, indigenous forms. Secondly, for years it was thought that the African was unfitted for technological knowledge and experience, and the education tended to be altogether classical, with a few rudimentary manual arts appended. The European reserved for himself the highly complicated, and, incidentally, the highly paid skilled jobs and information. Many Africans think this was a deliberate calculation, designed to withhold from the African the key to the exploitation of his own resources. Thirdly, it is true that most of the handwork, the drudgery that accompanies farming, house-building, and utensil-making, falls to the lot of the women. The man was the grand talker, the ruler, the schemer, the daring hunter and fighter. It has taken a long period of European occupation before the African could be involved in the hard work and long hours that accompany man's enslavement to the machine. Basic science studies, and the technological departments that apply these to Africa's vast and unfathomed resources, are the primary need of the university system of that continent.

If universities can be built with brick and stone, and attended by eager students, operated by proud faculty, then Africa is getting higher education. On more sober reflection, both friends and foes are likely to hold that this speedy acquisition of university-level education is just one more headache to add to Africa's troubles. It is well known that, like Rome, a university cannot be built in a day. For one thing, Africans are not available to staff them. And where "Africanization" has top priority in the mood of the day, this creates a problem of the first order. For another thing, the secondary schools are not established in order to feed these universities with properly trained students. For instance, we have indicated how, of the 127 Africans at Louvanium University in 1959, 121 were still engaged in their pre-university studies.

New movements are afoot to fill some of these gaps. The continent itself is taking more interest in supplying its own universities and scholarships. There is even some competition for the leadership in this contest. For instance, within the past two years, when Emperor Selassie offered the fifty All-Africa scholarships to his university, and to provide thirty more for students from South Africa, he was matched by President Tubman calling for regional co-operation in order to make the West Coast universities the best on the continent. Again, where West Nigeria has its magnificent plant, Premier Azikiwe of East Nigeria has been able to cajole funds and assistance from the United States, so that at the moment staff from the Universities of New Hampshire and of Michigan State are assisting him in the formation of his own. The new nation-states are taking pride in their own baby-institutions. When Sierre Leone was granted its university charter in 1960, the speaker laid claims to its becoming "a college for the educationally underprivileged of the West Coast: a West African Ruskin." Besides government subsidies for students, there are a few evidences of private support. The United African Company introduced in 1959 ten university scholarships, specifically for use in Africa. The Liberia Mining Company has agreed to endow a Tubman Chair of Health or Education at some West African institution, as well as to grant $30,000 annually for the expanded Monrovian campus. Firestone Company has agreed to give $25,000. In addition, some little outside assistance is available, as, for example, that furnished by the Phelps-Stokes Fund here in America. The British have a sizable scholarship program emanating from their colonial development promises made during World War II.

Besides the pride in more and more financial self-sufficiency, these fledgling universities are also producing their own scholars. Mostly, so far, they have distinguished themselves in the field of anthropological studies. And it is one of Africa's native sons who provides perhaps the best description of the prototype of educated leader most urgently needed in this hour:

When you say someone is an educated African, you mean that he is conscious of his people's problems, that he knows his culture well enough to be able to discriminate between its drawbacks and its advantages, that he can take the land his people have, the livestock his people keep, the wisdom that his elders teach, and the customs that his people follow, and, integrating all these with his Western knowledge and techniques, help to construct progressive African communities.[1]

That Kenya has such a product as Dr. Gikonyo wa Kiano who formulated this definition is a credit to its educational system.

A serious omission in advanced study in Africa is theological education (to which we shall refer later) and what we in America call "the Christian college." Although the latter has never been defined, and never finally stabilized, conversations about its primacy have occurred for a hundred years, covering the ground all the way between Catholic Newman's classic *The Idea of a University* to Quaker Elton Trueblood's current *The Idea of a College.* There is no need to summarize the theories justifying this essential ingredient of a free society at this point, but simply to report that Africa sadly lacks its existence or vision. The Christian university as a buffer institution would stand over against the utter socialization of education when controlled entirely by the state and over against the sectarianization of education when provided by religious groups, whether Roman Catholic or sectarian, whose purpose in both cases often is to inculcate a predigested set of religious ideas and customs. The claim implied in the title, *Christian* university, may be too great, but we remember that in the western world it is the great centers of independent research and free speech which have had the moral courage to withstand the assaults of the tyranny that comes, on the one hand, from the socialism with its uniformity of ideas imposed by the State, and on the other hand, from the sectarianism with its uniformity of ideas imposed by the Church —both claiming a monopoly of Truth. We would include under this blanket label the independently endowed university where religion is allowed an equal voice in the research, instruction, and life of the campus.

Whatever the form, it is this type of institution which Africa most needs to protect itself against the overweening nationalism, against the pretensions of superimposed scientism, and against the authoritarian dogmas of Church or communism. That these are real and present dangers I discovered to my dismay firsthand. In the Nigerian pre-election campaigns of December 1959, the so-called freedom elections, the opposing candidates debated, both with considerable misgivings, the freedom of the university. And rumors are abroad with what suspicion another Prime Minister regards his own country's university, perhaps the greatest in West Africa.

Or consider the following judgment of a leading authority, C. P. Groves, who in his monumental history, *The Planting of Christianity in Africa,* holds that

> The most insidious enemy, second to no other rival of the Christian faith in Africa, is the prevailing secularism of the West. African students, the leaders-to-be, studying at schools and universities in America and Europe, where the cult of scientific humanism gains prestige from the intellectual eminence of many who profess it, readily fall under its influence. The educated man, they may think they discover, has no need of religion. It is not an accident that political leaders of ability . . . are by no means necessarily Christian because first trained in mission schools.[2]

If that is the case for many of the Africans studying abroad, what can we expect when they return to establish the universities of Africa?

What we are saying is that here is a continent erecting an educational system without benefit of the Christian grounds and atmosphere upon which the university as we know it in the West was first born. In fact, it appears that religion on a par with the rest of the curriculum and the special training of the clergy in the broadest and highest education that has made him an influence in the West are both lacking. The following facts are among the reasons for this. One, the universities are being conceived and built too hurriedly, and in the shuffle the one element most likely omitted is religion. Two, the newer universities are largely the dreams of political leadership which may not be interested in religion. Three, the brand of faculty secured from local sources and that recruited from abroad is not necessarily religiously motivated; indeed, as has been observed, it may be highly secularized. When I raised the question of its omission with one principal, he equivocated, "Oh, yes, we would be glad to have a department of religious studies. Do you know of some rich American foundation that wishes to contribute one?" He knew as well as I that if "rich American foundations" were not responsible for the other integral departments, why should they supply the peripheral.

The impression ought not to be left that higher education in Africa is devoid of religion or is antireligious. The present complaint is that religion is not keeping up nor contributing its share during this determinative period. Nonetheless, there are signs that religion is alive if little more than a relic of that brought over in western dress. We can list these traditional manifestations.

First, there is the tradition of respect for perfunctory religion which most of the entering "chaps" bring from their preparatory schools. Drilled in the English "school boy" discipline, in so many cases, they have learned to snap their heels to attention, even at the religious exercises. Attending worship extends into the future with some of the loyalty that accompanies wearing the school tie. When Billy Graham asked the students assembled at the University of Ibadan how many were products of mission schools, every single hand arose.

Second, many campuses have chapels. I had the pleasure of addressing several, including the usual Sunday night service at Ft. Hare. But I could see there is a waning of interest. Nonetheless the majority have chapels, representing the cross-currents of faith. Protestants, Catholics, and Moslems have chapels at Makerere, and I was told the latter are pressing for a mosque at Ibadan, where the other two have imposing structures. Achimoto has chapels in the resident halls, chapels which have the interior appearance of high church Anglicanism but which in fact are available for other forms of worship. I discovered that it is only recently that the Moslem constituency insists on being represented. One wonders how soon the tide toward Africanism will resuscitate the appearance of tribal religion on a par with the world faiths.

Third, only a minority have departments of religion. Leading these would be Ghana, whereas Ibadan, Fourah Bay, and the Catholic universities offer some form of instruction in religion. Several have ventured into publications and convocations as ways of expressing this demand. Makerere ran extramural lectures in 1958 entitled "Religion and Society in East Africa" (later published). A more positive and experimental approach is taken at Achimoto and Ibadan. The former publishes a theological journal, as does Fourah Bay, and has pioneered a significant Easter series which has lately brought in Moslems along with the various Christian denominations for religious conversation. During the Christmas vacation of 1959 Ibadan staged a conference on "West African Religion." The brochure announcing the meetings read: "There is no aspect of West African culture that has been more misunderstood and misrepresented than West African forms of religion. Almost every word in the English language that is commonly used to describe African religion is a term of abuse: 'paganism,' 'fetishism,' 'idol worship' . . ." Perhaps a new day is dawning when self-criticism and appreciation can be shown for indigenous values in religion. It is along this line that the first number of the *Sierre Leone Bulletin of Religion,* June 1959, announced:

This is an attempt to provide a means of collecting and sifting information on the forms and history of religion, both Christian and non-Christian, within one fairly compact African territory.

That Africa provides a ready laboratory for the sociology of religion matched by few other places in the world has long been recognized; these are beginnings in the basic research. Several of the universities are exploring the possibility of comparative religion as the best approach to incorporating religion in the curriculum, and they would welcome outside assistance in bringing to their campuses authorities in "both (N.B.) western and eastern religions."

Fourth, there is a nucleus of some form of Christian student organization on each campus. This takes the expression of either an independent Christian Union such as at Makerere, or the Y, or the Student Christian Movement, or the Inter-Varsity Fellowship. The World Student Christian Federation held its first West African conference in 1958, and initiated its first African secretary in 1959. Liberia supplies the President of the World Alliance of YMCA's, and Nigeria has just gotten its first Y secretary. Nothing indigenous has appeared yet, and while these movements are invasions into Africa they do serve to link Africa with world thought and action among the collegiate generation.

These are some of the evidences that religion is present on the African campus, although its ferment is weak and stereotyped. The preceding survey does not lend itself to much hope. But what is more ominous is that those Africans, nursed through the beginnings of education in the mission school, and cast upon the mercies of the virtually secularized campus when they emerge through the rigorous qualifying screen, find little challenge in the local church when they return to the village. In the large village where I was stationed in East Nigeria I was given the list of nearly fifty local African leaders who had acquired degrees, at home or abroad. But not one attended church with any regularity or sustained interest. The casualty rate, the loss to the Church of the educated elite, is probably as high in Africa as anywhere in the world.

The imminent danger is that while the intellectual level of the pew is rising rapidly, that of the pulpit is deteriorating. As yet Makerere has not graduated a single candidate for the Christian ministry. This is almost the case at the other universities. The Christian ministry as it now functions in Africa just does not seem to attract the bright boys of new Africa. One fact that lends itself to the creation of a distinctly secular intellectual elite is the exceeding self-consciousness of the select few attending college. They know themselves as "the future leaders of Africa." Uprooted from their tribal homes and mission schools, they are fitting the mold of political and social agitators. White settlers in East Africa often attack Makerere, whose motto is "We build for the future," because "it puts ideas into their heads." The headmaster of the most celebrated high school in Kenya told me that Makerere is "the hell of our boys." (He apparently referred to their abandonment of the respectable conformity with which they were imbued by the mission schools—they go off to college only to become agitators and revolutionists!)

For another thing, the new nation-states are not likely to be as kindly disposed to missionaries predominating in higher education as was the case under the British colonial system in both East and West Africa. While the missionary is usually welcome to teach his technical subject, he must take a back seat in the life of the campus and university. Signs of the setback are already apparent, since at one university in West Africa the government scholarships for theological students (mostly those who are going out to teach in government schools) have been abruptly and unexplainably suspended.

Besides these two causes, the absence of an educated indigenous Christian ministry is due to some missions failing to recruit Africans, to educate them at the university level, and to provide them jobs and salaries equal to their countrymen with other degrees. When one calls to mind the random figures, such as the fact that only one Anglican clergyman has a degree in South Africa, only one Methodist has a degree in East Nigeria, and only two Baptists have degrees in West Nigeria—and these are among the oldest, most reliable of the mission bodies in Africa —one is inclined to lay the blame squarely at the feet of the missions. With all the highest administrative posts of the Church staffed with westerners, it was only natural that the African entering ecclesiastical service lived on starvation wages and was looked down on by his fellow citizens. Now the Church is in the predicament of trying to establish for the first time creditable theological education and to muster recruits in a social situation that has crystallized with a bias against the clergy. The East Africa Commission on Higher Theological Education which issued its report in 1959 hit the nail on the head:

The Church is losing the interest of the city people and the educated classes, the very groups which control the future of Africa, because it has no ministers capable of dealing with their problems and answering their questions. If the Church cannot provide theological education at the level of the highest intellectual life of the continent it will most certainly lose the mind of Africa.

The full account of this shocking vacuum of university-trained leadership within the African community itself has been fully documented in Yorke Allen's recently published survey of theological education in Africa and Asia. (See *A Seminary Survey*, Harper & Brothers, 1960.) While it was in the making, the International Missionary Council, alerted to this need, received several millions of dollars from the Rockefeller Foundation, to be matched by its own fund-raising, and has already begun to apply these monies to local needs in Africa and in Asia. However, I must say that with all the good promised by this belated start, neither the mission boards operating in Africa nor the indigenous Christians seem to be acting swiftly enough for this alarming predicament.

It thus appears that Christianity as related to education, with the mission schools passing into the hands of the nationalists, and the universities as secular as they are, faces its greatest challenge in the years immediately ahead. Dr. Emory Ross, the missionary leader who has paid twenty-five visits to Africa, asserts: "The situation is unprecedented and the rest of the world lacks experience in planning and aiding efficiently and speedily in ways acceptable."

The educationalism gripping Africa limps feebly, yet feverishly, in its flight. For while Africa has fallen for the philosophy that education is a cure-all, it pursues higher education without the wings to give it balanced sailing, namely, the wing of technology on the one hand, and the wing of theology on the other hand. There are persons who may question the propriety of the use of the analogy of the two wings, but there are few who would doubt that the educationalism of Africa must quickly discover a more sustaining propulsion and a worthier sense of direction. Christian thinking at the level of higher education in America could be of immeasurable help at this moment in Africa.

Footnotes

Chapter 1—tribalism

1. William Bascom and Melville J. Herskovits, *Continuity and Change in African Cultures*, p. 3. Chicago: The University of Chicago Press, 1959.
2. *Ibid.*
3. E. M. K. Mulira, *Thoughts of a Young African*, pp. 41-49. London: Lutterworth Press, 1945.
4. Camara Laye, *The African Child*, pp. 107, 135. Glasgow: Collins, 1959.
5. *Ibid.*
6. Mulira, *op. cit.*, p. 30.
7. Edwin W. Smith, *African Beliefs and Christian Faith*, p. 176. London: The United Society for Christian Literature, 1936.
8. *Ibid.*, p. 188.
9. L. S. Senghor, *Le Monde Noir*, No. 8-9, 1950, pp. 437 ff.
10. Mbonu Ojike, *My Africa*, p. 229. New York: The John Day Co., 1946.
11. Obefemi Owolowo, *The Path to Nigerian Freedom*, p. 18. London: Faber and Faber, 1947.
12. Quoted in George Wayland Carpenter, *The Way in Africa*, p. 114. New York: Friendship Press, 1959.
13. Ladislas Segy, "African Art: Its Culture," *Africa is Here*, p. 112. (Report of Africa Committee of the Division of Foreign Missions, National Council of the Churches of Christ in the U.S.A., published in New York, 1952.)
14. Quoted in *The West African Review*, June, 1960, p. 45.

Chapter 2—Islam

1. Vernon McKay, "Nationalism in British West Africa," *Foreign Policy Reports*, Vol. XXIV, No. 1, March 15, 1948, p. 7. New York: Foreign Policy Association, Incorporated.
2. John Scott, *Africa: World's Last Frontier*, p. 35. (Headline Series, No. 13, May, 1959.) New York: Foreign Policy Association, Inc., 1959.
3. J. Spencer Trimingham, *The Christian Church and Islam in West Africa*, p. 22. London: SCM Press Ltd, 1955.

Chapter 3—Christianity

1. Fernand Demany, *S O S Congo*, p. 83. Brussels, 1959.
2. M. A. C. Warren, *Caesar, the Beloved Enemy*, p. 59. Chicago: Alec R. Allenson, Inc., 1955.

3. For examples of this, confer V. Gordon Childe, *Social Evolution.* New York: Henry Schuman, 1951. See also Geoffrey Gorer, *Africa Dances.* Penguin Books, 1945.

4. Sir Francis Ibiam, *East Asia Christian Conference,* p. 11. (Privately printed, Calabar, East Nigeria, 1959.)

5. A. A. Nwafor Orizu, *Without Bitterness,* p. 161. New York: Creative Age Press, Inc., 1944.

6. Ojike, *My Africa,* p. 198.

7. D. Williams, *The Missions on the Eastern Frontier,* p. 553. (Doctoral dissertation filed with the University of Witwatersrand, South Africa, 1959.)

8. Walter Miller, *Have We Failed in Nigeria?,* p. 104. London: Lutterworth Press, 1947.

9. Emory Ross, *African Heritage,* pp. 12-13. New York: Friendship Press, 1952.

10. John Taylor, *Christianity and Politics in Africa,* p. 95. London: Penguin Books, 1957.

11. *Ibid.,* p. 102.

12. Ross, *op. cit.,* pp. 104, 106, 107.

Chapter 4—*nationalism*

1. Owolowo, *The Path to Nigerian Freedom,* p. 23.

2. Kwame Nkrumah, *Ghana,* p. 288. New York: Thomas Nelson & Sons, 1957.

3. *Ibid.*

4. Gamal Nasser, *Egypt's Liberation: The Philosophy of the Revolution,* pp. 109-111. Washington: Public Affairs Press, 1951.

5. George Padmore, *Pan-Africanism or Communism?,* p. 379. London: Dennis Dobson, 1956.

6. Ndabamingi Sithole, *African Nationalism,* p. 19. London: Oxford University Press, 1959.

7. *Ibid.,* p. 51.

8. Demany, *S O S Congo,* p. 96.

9. Church Mission Society Newsletter, London, May 1959.

10. Warren, *Caesar, the Beloved Enemy,* p. 67.

11. From C. Grove Haines, ed., *Africa Today,* pp. 14-16. Baltimore: The Johns Hopkins Press, 1955.

12. Chester Bowles, *Africa's Challenge to America,* p. 104. Berkeley: University of California Press, 1956.

13. Sithole, *op. cit.,* pp. 52-53.

14. Thomas Hodgkin, *Nationalism in Colonial Africa,* p. 98. New York: New York University Press, 1956.

15. George Shepperson, "The Politics of African Christian Separatist Movements," *African Affairs,* Vol. XXIV, No. 3, July 1954.

16. Hodgkin, *op. cit.,* p. 170.

17. Edward Roux, *Time Longer Than Rope,* p. 85. London: Gollancz, 1949.

18. Quoted in Daniel Thwaite, *The Seething African Pot,* pp. 37-38. London: Constable and Co., 1936.

19. Shepperson, *op. cit.*

20. Raymond Leslie Buell, *The Native Problem in Africa,* Vol. II, p. 605. New York: The Macmillan Company, 1928.

Chapter 5—*racism*

1. Albert Schweitzer, *On the Edge of the Primeval Forest*, p. 115. New York: The Macmillan Company, 1931.
2. Stuart Cloete, *The African Giant*, p. 235. Boston: Houghton Mifflin Company, 1955.
3. Quoted in J. J. Buskes, *South Africa's Policy of Apartheid*, p. 45. (Privately mimeographed, Heidelberg, South Africa, 1956.)
4. *The South African Observer*, Vol. V, No. 4, August 1959, p. 14.
5. Orizu, *Without Bitterness*, p. 299.
6. Trevor Shaw, *Through Ebony Eyes*, p. 20. London: Lutterworth Press, 1956.
7. John and Rena Karefa-Smart, *The Halting Kingdom*, pp. 71-72, 75. New York: Friendship Press, Inc., 1959.
8. Quoted in Buskes, *op. cit.*, p. 116.
9. Warren, *Caesar, the Beloved Enemy*, p. 74.

Chapter 6—*communism*

1. Padmore, *Pan-Africanism or Communism?*, pp. 339-340.
2. See Robert C. Good, "The Danger of Disillusionment with Africa," *Christianity and Crisis*, March 20, 1961, pp. 30-34.

Chapter 7—*educationalism*

1. Gikonyo wa Kiano, "East Africa: The Tug-of-War Continues," *Africa Is Here*, p. 30.
2. C. P. Groves, *The Planting of Christianity in Africa*, Vol. IV, p. 336. London: Lutterworth Press, 1948.